"MEASURING CHANGE: THE ART AND SCIENCE OF IMPACT ASSESSMENT"

A GUIDE TO IMPACT ASSESSMENT PROCESS

DR ANURAG TIWARI

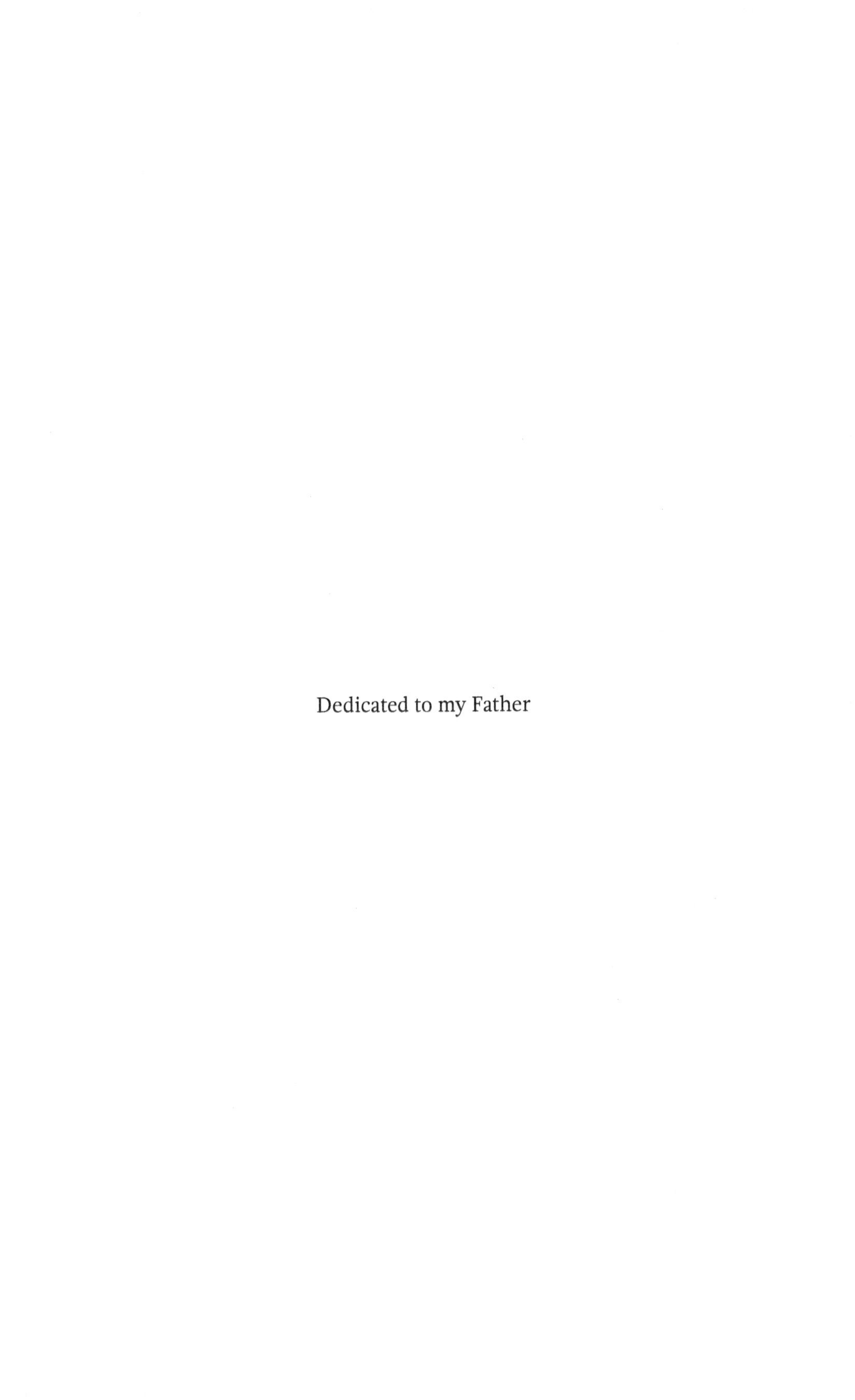

Dedicated to my Father

Contents

Foreword

In an era where sustainability, equity, and responsible governance are crucial to global progress, the role of impact assessment has never been more significant. Effective impact assessment serves as a cornerstone for informed decision-making, enabling policymakers, practitioners, and researchers to evaluate projects in a manner that fosters sustainable development and equitable resource distribution.

This book, Impact Assessment Methodology: A Comprehensive Guide, is a timely and much-needed resource that bridges the gap between theory and practice. It provides a structured understanding of impact assessment methodologies, covering environmental, social, economic, and health dimensions while integrating the latest advancements such as AI, big data analytics, gender and social inclusion strategies, and ESG frameworks.

What sets this book apart is its emphasis on practical application. By offering real-world case studies, evidence-based approaches, and step-by-step guidance, it equips readers with the necessary tools to conduct meaningful assessments across diverse sectors. Whether you are a student, researcher, policymaker, consultant, or corporate professional, this book offers valuable insights that cater to your specific needs and interests.

I commend the author for their dedication to compiling a comprehensive and accessible guide that will serve as an essential reference for years to come. As impact assessments continue to evolve, this book will undoubtedly be an indispensable resource for those striving to contribute to sustainable development and responsible governance.

It is with great pleasure that I introduce this book to you. I trust that it will not only enhance your understanding of impact assessments but also inspire you to apply these principles in ways that generate meaningful and lasting change.

Dr Bhagwati Charan

Preface

The journey of writing this book, Measuring the Change: The Art and Science of Impact Assessment has been one of deep exploration, collaboration, and a commitment to bridging the gap between theoretical concepts and practical applications. As impact assessments continue to play a critical role in ensuring sustainable development, informed decision-making, and equitable resource management, it became evident that there was a need for a structured and accessible resource to guide practitioners, researchers, policymakers, and students.

This book was born out of my experiences working in the field of impact assessment, witnessing firsthand the challenges and opportunities presented by diverse projects across environmental, social, economic, and governance domains. Throughout my career, I have engaged with professionals, academics, and development agencies, all of whom contributed valuable insights that have shaped the content of this work.

The primary objective of this book is to provide a holistic and practical guide to conducting effective impact assessments. It covers foundational principles, methodologies, and emerging trends such as AI, big data, and ESG frameworks. By incorporating real-world case studies and best practices, the book aims to empower readers with the knowledge and tools required to navigate complex impact assessment processes confidently.

I extend my sincere gratitude to all the experts, colleagues, and institutions that have supported this endeavor. Their contributions, feedback, and encouragement have been instrumental in bringing this book to fruition. Special thanks go to my mentors, peers, and family for their unwavering support and patience throughout this journey.

It is my hope that this book will serve as a valuable resource for anyone engaged in impact assessment, fostering critical thinking and promoting evidence-based approaches to sustainable development. May it inspire you to contribute to positive change in your projects, policies, and communities.

Dr Anurag Tiwari

Acknowledgements

This book is the result of collective effort, guidance, and support from many individuals and organizations who have played a crucial role in its development.

First and foremost, I would like to express my deepest gratitude to all the experts, practitioners, and academicians who have shared their invaluable knowledge and experiences in the field of impact assessment. Their insights and contributions have significantly enriched the content of this book.

I am especially thankful to my mentors and colleagues who provided constructive feedback, critical suggestions, and encouragement throughout the writing process. Their guidance helped ensure the book reflects both academic rigor and practical relevance.

I extend my sincere appreciation to the institutions and organizations whose resources, reports, and case studies have been referenced to illustrate real-world applications and best practices. Special thanks go to professionals from government agencies, international development organizations, and research institutions for sharing their expertise and data.

I am also grateful to my family and friends for their unwavering support, patience, and encouragement. Their belief in my work has been a constant source of motivation.

Finally, I thank the publishing team for their professionalism and dedication in bringing this book to life. Their attention to detail, design, and editorial support has been invaluable in creating a polished and accessible resource for readers.

To the readers of this book, I extend my heartfelt appreciation. It is my hope that this work empowers you to conduct impactful, sustainable, and meaningful assessments that contribute to positive change in your projects, organizations, and communities.

Thank you all for being a part of this journey

Prologue

Prologue

Impact assessment is more than just a regulatory requirement—it is a tool for shaping sustainable and equitable development. Throughout history, the consequences of uninformed decision-making have been evident in environmental degradation, social displacement, and economic inequalities. As the world faces increasing challenges such as climate change, resource depletion, and socio-economic disparities, the importance of robust impact assessments has become more pronounced than ever.

The evolution of impact assessment methodologies reflects a growing recognition of the need for comprehensive evaluation frameworks. From early environmental assessments to the integration of social and economic dimensions, the field has expanded significantly. Today, new frontiers such as artificial intelligence, big data analytics, and ESG frameworks are revolutionizing how impact assessments are conducted, making them more precise, inclusive, and forward-looking.

This book is designed to capture this evolution and serve as a practical guide for a broad audience, including students, researchers, policymakers, and professionals. It aims to provide a structured approach to understanding impact assessments, offering insights into key methodologies, case studies, and innovative strategies that can drive positive change.

As you delve into the chapters ahead, I encourage you to consider the broader implications of impact assessments. Beyond compliance and evaluation, they are instruments for safeguarding communities, protecting the environment, and fostering economic resilience. Whether you are new to the field or an experienced professional, this book will equip you with the knowledge and tools needed to conduct meaningful assessments and contribute to a more sustainable and equitable future.

[Dr Anurag Tiwari]

Abbreviations

- EIA - Environmental Impact Assessment
- SIA - Social Impact Assessment
- HIA - Health Impact Assessment
- EIA - Economic Impact Assessment
- IA - Impact Assessment
- ESG - Environmental, Social, and Governance
- CSR - Corporate Social Responsibility
- TBL - Triple Bottom Line
- LCA - Life Cycle Assessment
- SEA - Strategic Environmental Assessment
- CSR - Corporate Social Responsibility
- TBL - Triple Bottom Line
- PRA - Participatory Rural Appraisal
- UNFCCC - United Nations Framework Convention on Climate Change
- SDSN - Sustainable Development Solutions Network
- UNEP - United Nations Environment Programme
- IPCC - Intergovernmental Panel on Climate Change
- ADB - Asian Development Bank
- WB - World Bank
- GDP - Gross Domestic Product
- GHG - Greenhouse Gas
- UNSD - United Nations Statistical Division
- FAO - Food and Agriculture Organization
- SDGs - Sustainable Development Goals
- NBS - Nature-Based Solutions
- NGO - Non-Governmental Organization
- IFC - International Finance Corporation
- OECD - Organization for Economic Co-operation and Development
- IPR - Intellectual Property Rights
- PDD - Project Design Document
- MPA - Marine Protected Area
- IPBES - Intergovernmental Science-Policy Platform on Biodiversity and Ecosystem Services
- LULUCF - Land Use, Land-Use Change, and Forestry
- CER - Certified Emission Reduction

- FSC - Forest Stewardship Council
- EPA - Environmental Protection Agency
- R&D - Research and Development
- MCDA - Multi-Criteria Decision Analysis
- GPS - Global Positioning System
- UNDRIP - United Nations Declaration on the Rights of Indigenous Peoples
- FAO - Food and Agriculture Organization
- CBD - Convention on Biological Diversity
- UNHCR - United Nations High Commissioner for Refugees
- ADB - Asian Development Bank
- LULUC - Land Use, Land-Use Change
- GRI - Global Reporting Initiative
- SASB - Sustainability Accounting Standards Board
- UNESCO - United Nations Educational, Scientific and Cultural Organization
- COP - Conference of the Parties (UNFCCC)
- NDC - Nationally Determined Contributions
- CDM - Clean Development Mechanism
- REDD+ - Reducing Emissions from Deforestation and Forest Degradation
- FSC - Forest Stewardship Council
- NIR - National Inventory Report
- DOI - Department of the Interior
- ICSU - International Council for Science
- WWF - World Wildlife Fund
- IUCN - International Union for Conservation of Nature
- WBCSD - World Business Council for Sustainable Development
- IPCC - Intergovernmental Panel on Climate Change
- EPI - Environmental Performance Index
- OECD - Organization for Economic Co-operation and Development
- LEED - Leadership in Energy and Environmental Design
- ISO - International Organization for Standardization
- GCM - General Circulation Model
- BES - Biodiversity and Ecosystem Services
- SDP - Sustainable Development Plan
- ODS - Ozone-Depleting Substances
- SBT - Science-Based Target

1.1 What is Impact Assessment?

Impact Assessment (IA) refers to the systematic process of identifying, analyzing, and evaluating the potential impacts (positive or negative) of a proposed project, policy, or program on the environment, economy, society, and health. IA helps decision-makers understand the implications of their actions before implementation, ensuring that informed and balanced decisions are made.

Definition:

Impact assessment can be defined as:

"The process of evaluating the likely environmental, social, economic, and health impacts of a proposed project or policy, considering alternatives to mitigate or enhance those impacts."

1.2 Objectives of Impact Assessment

Impact Assessment (IA) is a critical tool designed to evaluate the consequences of proposed projects, policies, or programs. It helps predict potential outcomes, suggest mitigation measures, and ensure sustainability. The following are the key objectives of Impact Assessment, elaborated in detail:

1.2.1 To Predict Potential Outcomes of Proposed Activities

One of the fundamental objectives of impact assessment is to predict the likely consequences of a proposed activity before it is implemented. This proactive approach allows project developers, policymakers, and stakeholders to anticipate impacts on the environment, society, economy, and public health.

Why Prediction Matters?

By understanding potential outcomes in advance, decision-makers can:

Avoid unintended negative consequences.

Identify opportunities to maximize positive impacts.

Select the most sustainable and viable alternatives.

Tools and Techniques for Prediction:

Baseline Studies: Collecting current data on environmental, social, and economic conditions to assess potential changes.

Modeling and Simulations: Using tools like Geographic Information Systems (GIS), cost-benefit analysis (CBA), and environmental models to simulate project impacts.

Risk Assessments: Identifying and quantifying risks associated with specific project components.

Example:

For a proposed mining project, IA predicts impacts such as:

• Soil degradation and groundwater contamination.

• Loss of biodiversity and deforestation.

• Socio-economic outcomes like employment generation or displacement.

Such predictions help decision-makers weigh costs and benefits, enabling informed choices.

Long-Term Benefits of Prediction:

- Minimizes uncertainties associated with large-scale projects.

- Ensures the project's feasibility and acceptability.

- Enhances investor confidence and community trust.

- Predicting potential outcomes forms the foundation of impact assessment, ensuring that future projects are planned with foresight and preparedness

1.2.2To Propose Measures to Mitigate Negative Impacts and Enhance Positive Ones

Once the potential impacts of a proposed activity are identified and analyzed, the next objective of impact assessment is to suggest appropriate measures to mitigate negative impacts and enhance positive outcomes.

Understanding Mitigation:

Mitigation refers to actions or strategies aimed at:

- Avoiding negative impacts altogether.

- Minimizing the severity of unavoidable impacts.

- Restoring affected environments or communities.

- Compensating for unavoidable damages through alternative solutions.

Mitigation Strategies:

- Technical Measures: Designing eco-friendly infrastructure, reducing emissions, and adopting cleaner technologies.

- Policy Interventions: Introducing regulations to protect natural resources and vulnerable communities.

- Community Engagement: Collaborating with local stakeholders to ensure mitigation strategies are relevant and sustainable.

- Example:

In a highway construction project, proposed mitigation measures may include:

- Building wildlife corridors to protect animal movement.

- Using noise barriers to minimize disturbances for nearby communities.
- Implementing tree plantations to offset deforestation.

1.2. 3. To Provide a Structured Framework for Decision-Making

Impact assessment offers a systematic and structured framework that supports evidence-based decision-making. By following a clear methodology, it enables decision-makers to evaluate all potential options, ensuring the most suitable and sustainable choice is made.

Key Aspects of the Decision-Making Framework:

• **Transparency:** IA ensures an open and transparent process where stakeholders have access to relevant information.

• **Stakeholder Engagement:** Including voices of affected communities, local governments, and experts ensures decisions reflect diverse perspectives.

• **Accountability:** IA holds developers and policymakers accountable for their choices, requiring them to justify project approvals or rejections.

Components of the Framework:

• **Screening:** Determining if a project requires an IA.

• **Scoping:** Identifying key issues and potential areas of impact.

• **Impact Analysis:** Systematically evaluating the magnitude and significance of predicted impacts.

• **Alternatives Analysis:** Comparing project alternatives to choose the least harmful and most beneficial option.

• **Decision-Making:** Using IA findings to approve, modify, or reject a project.

- Example:

In a large-scale industrial project, IA provides a structured process to:

- Assess trade-offs between economic benefits and environmental risks.
- Compare alternatives, such as site locations, production technologies, or pollution management strategies.
- Present clear evidence to justify approvals, ensuring alignment with sustainability goals.

Benefits of a Structured Framework:

- Improves project efficiency and reduces delays.
- Ensures compliance with environmental laws and regulations.
- Facilitates stakeholder trust by ensuring fairness and clarity in decision-making.

In essence, IA provides a robust foundation for making informed, transparent, and well-documented decisions.

1.2.4. To Ensure Sustainable Development and Resource Management

Sustainability lies at the heart of impact assessments, as they aim to ensure that proposed activities meet the needs of the present without compromising the ability of future generations to meet their own needs.

I. Linking IA with Sustainability:

Impact assessments integrate environmental, social, and economic considerations to ensure long-term sustainability. This includes:

- Protecting natural ecosystems and biodiversity.
- Promoting equitable growth and social inclusion.
- Ensuring efficient use of natural resources.

II. Resource Management:

IA plays a critical role in managing resources responsibly by:

- Identifying potential over-exploitation of resources like land, water, and energy.
- Recommending measures to reduce waste, pollution, and degradation.
- Encouraging the adoption of circular economy principles.

III. Balancing Development with Conservation:

- IA ensures that development projects:
- Minimize harm to the environment.
- Address the needs of vulnerable communities.
- Contribute to economic growth without depleting resources.

Example:

In a renewable energy project (e.g., solar or wind farms), IA ensures:

- Minimal disruption to local biodiversity.
- Sustainable use of land resources without competing with agriculture.
- Community benefits such as employment, energy access, and capacity building.

1.2.5 Alignment with Global Goals:

IA directly supports the achievement of the United Nations' **Sustainable Development Goals (SDGs) by:**

- Promoting clean water and sanitation (SDG 6).
- Advancing sustainable cities and communities (SDG 11).
- Protecting life on land and underwater (SDG 14 and 15).
- Encouraging responsible consumption and production (SDG 12).

Long-Term Impact:

By integrating sustainability principles, IA ensures:

- Projects deliver benefits that extend beyond economic gains.
- Ecological systems remain resilient for future generations.
- Communities experience improved quality of life and equitable

development.

The objectives of Impact Assessment highlight its role as a critical tool for achieving sustainable, inclusive, and evidence-based development. By predicting potential outcomes, proposing mitigation strategies, providing a structured decision-making framework, and ensuring sustainable resource management, IA empowers policymakers, project developers, and stakeholders to make informed decisions that align with long-term sustainability goals.

These objectives are essential for balancing development priorities with environmental conservation and social well-being, ensuring that projects and policies contribute to a more sustainable and equitable future.

1.3 Key Principles of Impact Assessment:

The principles of Impact Assessment (IA) guide its implementation, ensuring that the process is effective, equitable, and scientifically sound. These principles act as the foundation for evaluating the environmental, social, economic, and health impacts of projects, policies, or programs. The following key principles are elaborated in detail:

1.3.1 Holistic Approach: Integration of Environmental, Social, Economic, and Health Considerations

The principle of a holistic approach ensures that impact assessment takes into account the interconnectedness of various dimensions of development, rather than focusing on a single aspect.

What Does Holistic Mean?

A holistic approach integrates:

Environmental considerations: Assessing the impact on air, water, soil, biodiversity, and ecosystems.

Social aspects: Evaluating effects on communities, culture, livelihoods, and quality of life.

Economic implications: Analyzing costs, benefits, job creation, income generation, and resource use.

Health outcomes: Examining direct and indirect effects on public health, such as pollution or disease prevalence.

Why is Integration Important?

- Impacts on one area often trigger cascading effects on others. For example, environmental degradation can lead to health problems, loss of livelihoods, and economic decline.

- Addressing these aspects together ensures that trade-offs and synergies are identified, leading to better decision-making.

- A holistic perspective promotes sustainability, ensuring that short-term gains do not undermine long-term environmental or societal health.

Example:

In a dam construction project:

The environmental assessment evaluates deforestation, water quality, and aquatic biodiversity loss.

The social assessment examines displacement of communities and cultural impacts.

The economic analysis identifies benefits like irrigation and power generation but also assesses costs such as relocation compensation.

The health assessment considers risks of waterborne diseases and access to clean drinking water.

By combining all dimensions, a holistic approach identifies balanced solutions that maximize positive outcomes while minimizing harm.

1.3.2 Participation: Engagement of Stakeholders to Ensure Transparency and Inclusivity

Participation is a cornerstone principle of Impact Assessment, ensuring that all stakeholders—especially those directly or indirectly affected by a project—are involved in the assessment process.

Why Participation Matters:

Inclusivity: Gives a voice to local communities, vulnerable groups, and marginalized populations.

Transparency: Builds trust in the decision-making process by ensuring open communication.

Ownership: Involving stakeholders encourages acceptance and ownership of project outcomes.

Local Knowledge: Community insights can complement scientific data, leading to better understanding and solutions.

Stakeholder Engagement Process:

Identification: Recognizing key stakeholders such as project-affected people, government agencies, NGOs, and experts.

Consultation: Conducting public hearings, focus group discussions, and surveys to gather feedback.

Incorporation: Integrating stakeholder feedback into decision-making, mitigation plans, and alternatives analysis.

Monitoring: Engaging stakeholders in follow-up assessments and post-implementation monitoring.

Example:

In a road development project through tribal areas:
Stakeholders such as tribal leaders, local communities, and NGOs should be consulted to understand cultural concerns, land ownership issues, and livelihood dependencies.
Their participation ensures solutions, such as bypass roads or compensation plans, are acceptable and sustainable.
Benefits of Participation:
Reduces conflicts and delays caused by resistance.
Promotes equitable decision-making, ensuring marginalized voices are heard.
Enhances project legitimacy and effectiveness.
1.3.3. Evidence-Based: Use of Scientific, Empirical, and Participatory Data for Analysis
An evidence-based approach emphasizes the use of credible, reliable, and verifiable data to inform impact assessment processes.
What Constitutes Evidence?
Scientific Data: Quantitative and qualitative data collected using established methods such as environmental modeling, health risk assessments, and economic analysis.
Empirical Data: Real-world observations, case studies, and experiences from similar projects.
Participatory Data: Information gathered through stakeholder consultations, surveys, and field visits.
Importance of Evidence-Based Analysis:
• Ensures accuracy and credibility of findings.
• Provides a rational basis for decision-making, reducing reliance on assumptions or anecdotal evidence.
• Enables comparisons between alternatives using measurable indicators.
• Enhances transparency, as decisions are grounded in documented data.
Tools for Evidence-Based Analysis:
• Environmental Models: Predicting impacts on air quality, water resources, and ecosystems.
• Cost-Benefit Analysis (CBA): Evaluating economic costs and benefits of proposed actions.
• Social Surveys: Capturing qualitative insights from affected communities.
• Geographic Information Systems (GIS): Mapping spatial impacts and land-use changes.

Example:

For a power plant project:

• Scientific studies assess air and water pollution levels.

• Empirical data from similar plants highlight health and economic impacts.

• Community consultations provide qualitative insights into public concerns.

• By combining these data sources, evidence-based analysis ensures that all impacts are accurately measured and effectively addressed.

1.3.4. Proactive: Addressing Impacts at the Planning Stage to Avoid Costly Remedial Measures Later

The principle of proactivity underscores the need to identify and address impacts during the planning and design stages of a project, rather than waiting to manage problems after they occur.

Why Proactivity is Essential:

• Prevention is often less expensive than mitigation or restoration.

• Early action reduces environmental damage, societal harm, and project delays.

• Proactive planning helps avoid legal and regulatory violations.

Proactive Measures in Impact Assessment:

• Early Screening: Identifying projects that require detailed assessments to minimize future risks.

• Scoping: Determining significant impacts early in the process to prioritize key issues.

• Alternatives Analysis: Assessing different project options to select the least harmful and most sustainable approach.

• Mitigation Planning: Integrating preventive measures into project design, such as adopting green technologies or avoiding ecologically sensitive areas.

• Example:

In an urban infrastructure project:

• A proactive IA would identify risks such as traffic congestion, increased pollution, and community displacement.

• Solutions like eco-friendly transportation systems, noise barriers, and resettlement plans can be incorporated at the planning stage.

This approach avoids costly remedial actions, such as lawsuits, retrofits, or project shutdowns.

Benefits of Proactive Impact Assessment:

• Enhances project efficiency and cost-effectiveness.

• Minimizes adverse impacts on the environment and society.

• Improves public perception and trust in the project.

The key principles of Impact Assessment—holistic approach, participation, evidence-based analysis, and proactivity—ensure that the assessment process is comprehensive, inclusive, scientifically sound, and forward-looking. By adhering to these principles, Impact Assessment helps projects and policies achieve long-term sustainability while minimizing harm and maximizing benefits for society, the economy, and the environment.

These principles not only guide the technical process of IA but also build trust, transparency, and accountability among stakeholders, leading to better outcomes for all.

1.4 Historical Context and Evolution of Impact Assessments

Impact Assessment has its roots in the environmental movement of the 1960s and 1970s, which emphasized the need for sustainable development and environmental protection.

1.4.1 Early Beginnings:

1969: The National Environmental Policy Act (NEPA) in the United States introduced the first formal Environmental Impact Assessment (EIA) framework.

NEPA emphasized the need to assess environmental impacts before project implementation and laid the foundation for global environmental governance.

1.4.2.International Developments:

The adoption of EIA procedures became widespread globally, driven by the United Nations and international development organizations like the World Bank and Asian Development Bank (ADB).

Countries started implementing their EIA frameworks as part of legal mandates.

1.4.3 Expanding Scope:

In the 1980s-1990s, other types of impact assessments emerged, including Social Impact Assessments (SIA) and Health Impact Assessments (HIA).

The 21st century saw the introduction of Strategic Environmental Assessments (SEA) for policies and programs.

Modern assessments also integrate gender equality, climate change, and socio-economic considerations.

1.5 Types of Impact Assessments

Impact Assessment has diversified to address specific concerns across different domains. The major types of impact assessments include:

1.5.1 Environmental Impact Assessment (EIA)

Definition: EIA is a process that evaluates the environmental consequences of a proposed project or development.

Key Components:

Assessment of air, water, soil quality.

Biodiversity impacts.

Waste and pollution management.

Process:

1.5.2 Social Impact Assessment (SIA)

Definition: SIA evaluates the social consequences of a proposed development or policy, focusing on communities, culture, and livelihoods.

Key Components:

• Resettlement and displacement.

• Impact on vulnerable groups.

• Access to services like education and healthcare.

Tools: Participatory approaches, surveys, focus groups, and stakeholder engagement.

Example: SIA for a large dam project analyzing relocation impacts on tribal populations.

1.5.3 Economic Impact Assessment

Definition: Economic Impact Assessments measure the financial and economic consequences of a proposed project.

Key Components:

• Cost-Benefit Analysis (CBA).

• Employment generation.

• Effects on local businesses and regional economies.

Tools: Input-output models, economic multipliers, and statistical tools.

Example: Economic assessment for a new industrial zone's effect on job creation.

1.5.4 Health Impact Assessment (HIA)

Definition: HIA assesses the potential health impacts of a project or policy, ensuring public health is prioritized.

Key Components:

• Air and water quality impacts health.

• Disease spread and occupational hazards.

• Mental health and well-being.

Tools: Epidemiological studies, health indicators, and risk assessments.

Example: HIA for a mining project evaluating air quality impacts on respiratory health.

1.5.5 Strategic Environmental Assessment (SEA)

Definition: SEA is applied at a policy, plan, or program level to integrate environmental considerations into strategic decision-making.

Key Components:

• Long-term sustainability goals.

• Cumulative impacts of multiple projects.

Example: SEA for a national transportation policy assessing large-scale environmental impacts.

1.6 Importance of Impact Assessments in Policy and Projects

Impact Assessments play a crucial role in ensuring sustainability, transparency, and responsible development. Their importance can be highlighted across the following dimensions:

1.6.1.Environmental Protection

• IA helps safeguard ecosystems and natural resources.

• Ensures compliance with national and international environmental regulations.

• Mitigates harmful impacts such as deforestation, pollution, and biodiversity loss.

1.6.2. Informed Decision-Making

• IA provides decision-makers with data-driven insights.

• Balances economic development with social and environmental priorities.

• Encourages adoption of alternatives that minimize adverse impacts.

1.6.3. Risk Mitigation

• Identifies potential risks early in the planning phase.

• Reduces project delays, cost overruns, and conflicts with stakeholders.

• Enhances project credibility and acceptance.

1.6.4. Social Inclusion and Equity

• Promotes participation of affected communities in decision-making processes.

• Addresses concerns of vulnerable groups, ensuring equity and gender sensitivity.

• Mitigates negative impacts like displacement, livelihood loss, and inequality.

1.6.5. Economic Efficiency

• Optimizes resource allocation through cost-benefit analysis.

• Enhances local economic opportunities and long-term benefits.

• Attracts funding by ensuring compliance with development standards.

1.6.6. Policy Integration and Sustainability

• Aligns projects and policies with Sustainable Development Goals (SDGs).

• Ensures long-term environmental, social, and economic sustainability.

• Strengthens governance and accountability mechanisms.

1.7 Conclusion

This chapter has introduced the concept, history, and various types of impact assessments, highlighting their critical role in balancing development goals with environmental protection, social well-being, and economic growth. Impact Assessments have evolved as indispensable tools for promoting sustainable and inclusive development, enabling policymakers, practitioners, and stakeholders to make well-informed decisions.

The subsequent chapters will delve deeper into methodologies, tools, case studies, and innovations in impact assessments to provide a comprehensive understanding of this essential process.

CHAPTER II

Impact Assessment (IA) serves as a bridge between theoretical understanding and practical application, enabling policymakers, project developers, and stakeholders to anticipate, evaluate, and address potential consequences of development projects. The theoretical foundations of IA provide a structured framework that ensures sustainable outcomes, integrates diverse perspectives, and aligns with broader global objectives like the Sustainable Development Goals (SDGs). This chapter explores the conceptual frameworks, principles, stakeholder engagement, and connections to sustainability that underpin IA.

2.1 Conceptual Frameworks for Impact Assessments

Conceptual frameworks for Impact Assessment establish a structured approach to analyzing the potential impacts of proposed activities. These frameworks define the scope, methodologies, and objectives, offering clarity and direction throughout the IA process.

2.1.1 Pressure-State-Response (PSR) Framework

The Pressure-State-Response (PSR) framework is a widely recognized conceptual model that helps analyze the dynamic relationship between human activities and environmental impacts. Developed by the Organisation for Economic Co-operation and Development (OECD), this framework is instrumental in environmental assessment and policy-making processes. By categorizing environmental interactions into three interconnected components—Pressure, State, and Response—it provides a systematic approach to identify, evaluate, and manage environmental challenges.

2.1.2 Overview of the PSR Framework

The PSR framework operates on a cause-effect-response model that links human activities to environmental conditions and the subsequent measures taken to address the changes. This cycle emphasizes how anthropogenic actions drive environmental changes and how societies react to these changes to promote sustainability.

2.1.2.1 Pressure

Definition: Pressures are the human-induced factors that exert stress on natural ecosystems and environmental resources. These factors include both direct activities, such as deforestation or industrial emissions, and indirect influences, such as population growth and urbanization.

Examples:

• Industrial emissions contribute to air pollution.

• Agricultural runoff leading to water contamination.

• Overfishing affects marine biodiversity.

2.1.2.2 State

Definition: The state represents the condition of the environment as influenced by the identified pressures. This includes measurable changes in air, water, soil, and biodiversity that signify the health of ecosystems.

Examples:

• Elevated levels of greenhouse gases in the atmosphere.

• Declining fish populations in overexploited oceans.

• Increased soil erosion due to deforestation.

2.1.2.3 Response

Definition: Responses are the strategies, policies, and actions implemented to address environmental changes and reduce pressures. These measures aim to restore balance, mitigate negative impacts, and promote sustainability.

Examples:

• Adoption of renewable energy technologies to reduce carbon emissions.

• Establishment of marine protected areas to conserve biodiversity.

• Implementation of sustainable agricultural practices to prevent soil degradation.

2.1.3 Detailed Exploration of PSR Components

I. Pressure: Drivers of Environmental Stress

Pressures arise from various human activities that demand natural resources or produce waste. Understanding these pressures is the first step toward mitigating their impact.

i. Types of Pressures:

• Pollution: Emissions of harmful substances into the air, water, and soil.

• Resource Exploitation: Overuse of renewable and non-renewable resources, such as fossil fuels and forests.

• Land-Use Changes: Urbanization, agriculture, and industrial expansion.

ii. Key Drivers of Pressures:

• Economic development, leading to higher resource consumption.

• Population growth, increasing the demand for land, water, and energy.

• Technological advancements that intensify resource extraction.

II. State: Assessing Environmental Conditions

The state reflects the current health and functionality of ecosystems. Monitoring environmental states helps track the impact of pressures over time.

i. Indicators of Environmental State:

• Air Quality: Levels of pollutants like PM2.5, sulfur dioxide, and nitrogen oxides.

• Water Quality: Concentrations of nitrates, phosphates, and heavy metals in water bodies.

• Biodiversity: Population trends of species and the extent of natural habitats.

ii. Importance of State Monitoring:

• Helps establish environmental baselines for comparative analysis.

• Identifies priority areas for intervention and resource allocation.

III. Response: Actions to Address Environmental Changes

Responses are the measures implemented by governments, organizations, and communities to mitigate or reverse environmental degradation.

i. Types of Responses:

• Policy and Regulation: Enacting laws to limit emissions and protect natural areas.

• Technological Innovations: Developing cleaner production methods and renewable energy sources.

• Public Awareness and Education: Promoting sustainable practices among individuals and communities.

ii. Examples of Effective Responses:

• International agreements like the Kyoto Protocol and Paris Agreement on climate change.

• National policies for waste management and recycling.

• Local initiatives for afforestation and sustainable farming.

2.1.4 Application of the PSR Framework in Environmental Impact Assessments

The PSR framework is particularly useful in Environmental Impact Assessments (EIAs), where it serves as a guiding tool to identify and evaluate environmental challenges and their solutions. Below are its applications in monitoring pollution and planning sustainable interventions:

I. Monitoring Pollution

I. Air Pollution:

• Pressure: Emissions from industrial processes, vehicles, and power plants.

• State: Poor air quality indices, higher levels of particulate matter, and ozone depletion.

• Response: Implementation of stricter emission standards and transition to renewable energy sources.

II. Water Pollution:

• Pressure: Discharge of untreated sewage, industrial effluents, and agricultural runoff.

• State: Contaminated water bodies, reduced oxygen levels, and eutrophication.

• Response: Construction of wastewater treatment plants and promotion of organic farming practices.

III. Soil Pollution:

• Pressure: Use of chemical fertilizers, pesticides, and industrial waste dumping.

• State: Declining soil fertility, increased salinity, and heavy metal accumulation.

• Response: Adoption of sustainable agriculture and soil remediation techniques.

II. Biodiversity Conservation

• Pressure: Habitat destruction, climate change, and introduction of invasive species.

• State: Loss of species diversity and ecosystem services.

• Response: Establishment of wildlife corridors, restoration of degraded ecosystems, and enforcement of conservation laws.

i. Sustainable Resource Management

• Pressure: Overexploitation of resources like water, minerals, and forests.

• State: Depletion of aquifers, loss of forest cover, and desertification.

• Response: Promotion of water-saving technologies, afforestation drives, and resource recycling.

2.1.5 Strengths of the PSR Framework

• Systematic Approach:

Facilitates structured analysis of environmental challenges.

• Cause-Effect Relationship:

Highlights the linkages between human activities and environmental impacts.

• Adaptability:

Applicable to diverse environmental contexts and scales.

• Action-Oriented:

Focuses on developing practical solutions to mitigate pressures.

2.1.6 Limitations of the PSR Framework

i. Simplistic Representation:

May oversimplify complex ecological and socio-economic interactions.

ii. Data Dependency:

Requires comprehensive data for accurate assessment and planning.

iii. Focus on Responses:

May neglect underlying systemic issues in favor of immediate solutions.

The PSR framework is an invaluable tool for understanding and managing the interactions between human activities and the environment. By providing a clear and structured approach, it enables policymakers and stakeholders to identify pressures, evaluate environmental states, and implement effective responses. While it has limitations, its strengths make it a cornerstone of Environmental Impact Assessments and a key contributor to sustainable development.

2.1.7 Risk Assessment Framework

The Risk Assessment Framework is a structured approach used to evaluate the likelihood and severity of adverse outcomes resulting from specific activities or exposures. Rooted in scientific methodology, this framework aids in decision-making processes by providing a systematic analysis of potential risks. It is widely applied across disciplines such as environmental science, public health, engineering, and economics, with a particularly notable role in Health Impact Assessments (HIA).

I. Overview of the Risk Assessment Framework

The framework consists of four critical components: hazard identification, exposure assessment, risk characterization, and risk management. Each stage builds on the preceding one to ensure a thorough evaluation of risks associated with human activities or projects.

II. Hazard Identification:

• Definition: Identifying agents, activities, or scenarios capable of causing harm to humans, ecosystems, or infrastructure.

• Examples: Toxic chemicals, biological pathogens, natural disasters, or workplace hazards.

III. Exposure Assessment:

• Definition: Quantifying the extent and duration of exposure to identified hazards, considering factors such as population groups, geography, and time frames.

• Examples: Determining levels of air pollutant exposure for residents near an industrial zone.

IV. Risk Characterization:

• Definition: Combining hazard and exposure data to estimate the probability and magnitude of adverse outcomes.

Examples: Estimating the likelihood of respiratory illnesses in a population due to air pollution.

v. Risk Management:

• Definition: Implementing strategies to mitigate, transfer, or accept risks based on assessment outcomes.

Examples: Enforcing emission regulations, public health campaigns, or emergency preparedness plans.

2.1.8 Detailed Exploration of Framework Components

i. Hazard Identification

Hazard identification is the foundation of risk assessment. It involves recognizing all potential sources of harm, their characteristics, and the mechanisms through which they may cause damage.

Types of Hazards:

• Chemical Hazards: Exposure to substances such as lead, asbestos, or pesticides.

• Biological Hazards: Infections caused by bacteria, viruses, or fungi.

• Physical Hazards: Noise, radiation, or extreme weather events.

• Social and Behavioral Hazards: Poor living conditions, stress, or lifestyle choices.

Key Steps in Hazard Identification:

• Data Collection: Gathering information on known hazards from scientific literature, databases, and monitoring systems.

• Mechanism Analysis: Understanding how the hazard interacts with biological, environmental, or structural systems to cause harm.

ii. Exposure Assessment

Exposure assessment evaluates who is exposed to the hazard, how, and to what extent. It considers factors such as duration, frequency, and intensity of exposure.

Components of Exposure Assessment:

• Source Identification: Determining the origin of the hazard (e.g., industrial emissions).

• Pathway Analysis: Mapping the routes through which the hazard reaches the target population (e.g., air, water, soil, or food).

• Receptor Analysis: Identifying the affected populations, including vulnerable groups like children or the elderly.

Methods of Exposure Assessment:

• Direct Monitoring: Measuring concentrations of pollutants or toxins in the environment.

• Modeling Approaches: Using computational models to estimate exposure based on known variables.

• Survey-Based Methods: Gathering self-reported data on exposure patterns.

2.1.9 Application in Health Impact Assessments (HIA)

The Risk Assessment Framework is integral to Health Impact Assessments (HIA), where it evaluates potential public health risks associated with projects, policies, or activities. Below are its applications:

I. Evaluating Exposure to Toxic Substances

• Scenario: Assessing the health impacts of a proposed industrial facility.

• Hazard Identification: Identifying pollutants like sulfur dioxide, benzene, and heavy metals.

• Exposure Assessment: Measuring expected pollutant concentrations near residential areas.

• Risk Characterization: Estimating increased cancer risks or respiratory illnesses.

• Risk Management: Recommending pollution controls or buffer zones.

II. Addressing Disease Outbreak Risks

• Scenario: Analyzing risks of waterborne diseases in a flood-prone region.

• Hazard Identification: Recognizing pathogens such as E. coli and cholera bacteria.

• Exposure Assessment: Assessing contamination levels in drinking water sources.

• Risk Characterization: Estimating infection rates and potential fatalities.

• Risk Management: Suggesting water treatment facilities and emergency response plans.

III. Managing Risks in Urban Development

• Scenario: Evaluating health impacts of urban housing projects.

• Hazard Identification: Identifying risks like air pollution, traffic accidents, and lack of green spaces.

• Exposure Assessment: Analyzing how residents will be exposed to these risks.

• Risk Characterization: Determining the likelihood of adverse health outcomes.

• Risk Management: Designing safer traffic systems, increasing urban greenery, and monitoring air quality.

• Strengths of the Risk Assessment Framework

• Structured Process: Ensures comprehensive evaluation of potential risks.

• Scientific Basis: Relies on empirical data and evidence-based methodologies.

• Transparency: Clearly communicates risks and uncertainties to stakeholders.

• Versatility: Applicable across diverse sectors and disciplines.

• Challenges and Limitations

• Data Gaps: Incomplete or unreliable data can affect the accuracy of assessments.

• Complex Interactions: Simplifying complex systems may overlook indirect or cumulative effects.

• Uncertainty: Assumptions and models introduce uncertainty in risk estimates.

• Resource Intensity: Conducting detailed assessments requires significant time, expertise, and funding.

The Risk Assessment Framework is a powerful tool for understanding and managing potential risks across various domains. By systematically analyzing hazards, exposure, and potential outcomes, it enables stakeholders to make informed decisions and implement effective strategies. Its application in Health Impact Assessments exemplifies its value in protecting public health and promoting sustainable development. Despite its challenges, the framework remains a cornerstone of risk management and decision-making processes.

2.2 Social Frameworks in Impact Assessment

Social frameworks are integral to understanding how development projects and policies influence communities. By focusing on social, cultural, and economic dimensions, these frameworks help identify potential risks and opportunities associated with proposed activities. They ensure that projects promote social equity, safeguard livelihoods, and minimize cultural disruptions, thereby fostering sustainable and inclusive development.

This elaboration explores key aspects of social frameworks, emphasizing their principles, components, and application in assessing community-level impacts.

I. Understanding Social Frameworks

Social frameworks serve as tools to assess the potential effects of development initiatives on individuals, households, and communities.

These frameworks examine the interplay between social structures, human capital, and external interventions to ensure that outcomes align with principles of equity, justice, and sustainability.

Key Objectives:

• Protecting Livelihoods: Ensuring that projects do not jeopardize community incomes and employment.

• Preserving Culture: Mitigating disruptions to traditions, values, and identity.

• Promoting Equity: Ensuring fair distribution of benefits and addressing power imbalances.

• Core Dimensions of Social Frameworks

a. Livelihood Impacts

Livelihoods form the foundation of community well-being. Projects can disrupt income sources, alter employment patterns, or affect resource availability.

Key Considerations:

• Economic Dependency: Identifying populations reliant on specific resources or sectors (e.g., fishing communities affected by dam construction).

• Vulnerability: Assessing the resilience of marginalized groups to livelihood disruptions.

• Alternative Livelihoods: Proposing viable substitutes to mitigate adverse impacts.

• Examples of Livelihood Impacts:

- Infrastructure projects displacing communities dependent on agriculture or forestry.

- Industrial activities reducing access to traditional fishing grounds.

b. Cultural Disruptions

Cultural heritage is vital to community identity and cohesion. Development projects can unintentionally erode traditions, disrupt social bonds, or impact sacred sites.

Key Considerations:

• Cultural Sensitivity: Recognizing the significance of local customs, rituals, and heritage.

• Community Engagement: Involving affected groups in decision-making to respect cultural values.

• Mitigation Measures: Avoiding or compensating for impacts on culturally significant locations.

• Examples of Cultural Disruptions:
- Urbanization projects encroaching on indigenous sacred sites.
- Infrastructure developments altering traditional settlement patterns.

c. Social Equity

Equity ensures that all groups, especially marginalized and vulnerable populations, benefit from development projects without bearing disproportionate burdens.

Key Considerations:

• Inclusion: Ensuring participation of women, minorities, and disadvantaged groups in planning and implementation.

• Fair Distribution: Addressing disparities in access to project benefits.

• Conflict Resolution: Mediating tensions between stakeholders to promote harmonious outcomes.

• Examples of Equity Challenges:
- Unequal access to compensation packages in land acquisition projects.
- Power imbalances leading to elite capture of resources.

d. The Sustainable Livelihood Framework (SLF)

The Sustainable Livelihood Framework (SLF) is a widely adopted tool for evaluating how projects impact human, social, physical, financial, and natural capital. Developed by the UK's Department for International Development (DFID), the SLF provides a holistic approach to analyzing community resilience and vulnerabilities.

Components of SLF:

• Human Capital: Skills, knowledge, health, and labor capacity of individuals.

• Social Capital: Social networks, trust, and support systems within a community.

• Physical Capital: Infrastructure, tools, and resources essential for productivity.

• Financial Capital: Income, savings, and access to credit or financial services.

• Natural Capital: Access to land, water, forests, and other environmental resources.

Application of SLF:

The SLF examines how external factors (e.g., policies, institutions, and shocks) influence these capitals, enabling a comprehensive understanding of project impacts.

Detailed Exploration of SLF Components

1. Human Capital

Human capital determines a community's capacity to adapt to change and seize opportunities.

• Positive Impacts:

- Training programs improving skills and employability.
- Health infrastructure reducing disease burden.

• **Negative Impacts:**

- Displacement disrupting access to education or healthcare.
- Loss of skilled workers due to migration.

2. Social Capital

- Social capital enhances community resilience by fostering collaboration and mutual support.

• Positive Impacts:

- Projects strengthening community networks through participatory processes.
- Enhanced trust in institutions via transparent decision-making.

• **Negative Impacts:**

- Conflicts arising from unequal distribution of benefits.
- Erosion of traditional support systems due to cultural disruption.

3. Physical Capital

Physical infrastructure is critical for accessing markets, services, and opportunities.

• Positive Impacts:

- Roads and bridges improving connectivity and economic prospects.
- Housing projects enhancing living standards.

• **Negative Impacts:**

- Large-scale developments displacing communities.
- Poorly designed infrastructure causing environmental degradation.

4. Financial Capital

Financial resources enable communities to invest in development and absorb shocks.

• **Positive Impacts:**

- Compensation packages for displaced individuals.
- Access to microfinance for small businesses.

• **Negative Impacts:**

- Unequal compensation creating tensions among stakeholders.
- Debt burdens from poorly planned financial interventions.

5. Natural Capital

Natural resources support livelihoods, especially in rural and indigenous communities.

• **Positive Impacts:**

- Conservation initiatives enhancing resource sustainability.

- Projects promoting renewable energy and biodiversity.

• **Negative Impacts:**

- Overexploitation of resources leading to environmental degradation.

- Restricted access to traditional lands and waters.

II. Application of Social Frameworks in Impact Assessment

1. Infrastructure Development

Scenario: Building a new highway through rural communities

Infrastructure projects, such as highways, serve as catalysts for economic growth and connectivity. However, they also present significant social challenges, particularly in rural settings where livelihoods, cultural practices, and equity dynamics are intricately linked to the local environment.

Impacts:

• **Livelihood:** The construction of a highway often necessitates land acquisition, leading to the displacement of farmers and loss of access to agricultural land. For rural communities reliant on subsistence farming, this can mean a direct loss of income and food security. Additionally, secondary impacts may include reduced access to local markets and disruption of traditional economic activities such as livestock grazing or small-scale enterprises.

• **Culture:** Increased urbanization and connectivity can disrupt traditional practices and social norms. For instance, the introduction of external influences may lead to the erosion of indigenous knowledge, local dialects, and rituals. Cultural festivals tied to specific locations might be rendered infeasible if those areas are disrupted by construction.

• **Equity:** Compensation and resettlement often disproportionately benefit wealthier landowners who possess legal documentation for their properties. Marginalized groups, such as tenant farmers or landless laborers, frequently receive inadequate or no compensation. This exacerbates pre-existing inequities, leaving vulnerable populations worse off.

Mitigation:

• Inclusive Consultation Processes: Engage all stakeholders, including marginalized groups, in the planning and decision-making process. Participatory approaches ensure that diverse voices are heard, fostering transparency and trust.

• **Alternative Livelihood Programs:** Develop initiatives to provide skills training, financial support, and employment opportunities for affected individuals. For example, establishing cooperatives for displaced farmers to access new agricultural lands or diversifying income sources through non-farm activities.

2. Industrial Projects

Scenario: Establishing a mining operation near indigenous lands

Industrial development, while pivotal for national economies, often places immense strain on the social and environmental fabric of host communities, particularly indigenous populations. Mining operations bring unique challenges due to their intrusive nature and long-term ecological consequences.

Impacts:

• **Livelihood:** Indigenous communities frequently depend on natural resources for their sustenance and cultural practices. Mining operations can result in restricted access to forests, rivers, and other critical resources. This loss diminishes traditional livelihoods such as hunting, fishing, and small-scale farming.

• Culture: Sacred sites, often tied to indigenous cosmologies, are at risk of desecration. Traditional knowledge, passed down through generations, may lose relevance as communities adapt to external economic pressures.

• **Equity:** Benefits of mining, such as employment opportunities or revenue sharing, are often concentrated among external stakeholders, such as multinational corporations or urban elites. Local communities may bear the brunt of environmental degradation without equitable compensation or reinvestment.

Mitigation:

• **Agreements Ensuring Local Benefits:** Negotiate community development agreements (CDAs) that guarantee revenue sharing, local hiring, and investment in public infrastructure like schools and healthcare facilities.

• **Preservation of Cultural Heritage:** Collaborate with indigenous leaders to map and safeguard sacred sites. Support initiatives to document and promote traditional knowledge, ensuring its transmission to future generations.

3. Urban Expansion

Scenario: Expanding a city into peri-urban areas

Urbanization is a global trend that often encroaches upon peri-urban areas, transforming the livelihoods and social structures of these transitional zones. While urban expansion can offer new opportunities, it also presents complex social challenges.

Impacts:

• **Livelihood:** Small-scale farmers are frequently displaced as agricultural lands are converted into residential or commercial zones. The transition from rural to urban economies can be particularly challenging for those lacking the skills or resources to adapt.

• **Culture:** Traditional lifestyles, including communal practices and local governance structures, often erode under urban influences. Peri-urban residents may struggle to integrate into urban settings, leading to a loss of cultural identity and social cohesion.

• **Equity:** Vulnerable groups, including migrants, women, and informal workers, are often excluded from decision-making processes. This exclusion results in inequitable access to resources such as affordable housing, public transportation, and essential services.

Mitigation:

• **Affordable Housing Initiatives:** Design and implement policies that provide low-cost housing options for displaced families. Incorporating inclusive urban planning ensures equitable access to basic amenities and prevents the formation of slums.

• **Policies Supporting Urban-Rural Linkages:** Strengthen rural supply chains and promote peri-urban agriculture to maintain economic and cultural ties between urban centers and surrounding areas.

Strengths of Social Frameworks

• **Holistic Approach:** Social frameworks address a wide range of impacts, from economic displacement to cultural preservation, ensuring comprehensive assessments that consider diverse dimensions of community well-being.

• **Inclusivity:** By promoting stakeholder participation, these frameworks empower communities to voice their concerns and influence outcomes. Inclusivity fosters accountability and mitigates resistance.

• **Sustainability:** Aligning project outcomes with long-term community goals enhances resilience. For instance, integrating environmental conservation into infrastructure projects ensures sustainable development that benefits future generations.

Challenges and Limitations

• **Complexity:** Social impacts are multifaceted and interconnected, requiring expertise in sociology, anthropology, and economics. The interdependence of various factors complicates the assessment and mitigation process.

• **Subjectivity:** Cultural and social factors, such as identity, belonging, and well-being, are inherently subjective and difficult to quantify. This subjectivity can lead to variations in interpretation and prioritization of impacts.

• **Time and Resources:** Comprehensive social impact assessments (SIAs) demand significant time, financial investment, and human resources. Balancing thoroughness with practical constraints remains a persistent challenge.

Applying social frameworks in impact assessment is crucial for mitigating adverse effects and ensuring equitable and sustainable outcomes. While challenges such as complexity, subjectivity, and resource constraints persist, the strengths of these frameworks—holistic analysis, inclusivity, and alignment with long-term goals—underscore their value in contemporary development projects. Effective application requires a commitment to participatory processes, cross-disciplinary expertise, and adaptive strategies that address the evolving needs of impacted communities.

Social frameworks, particularly tools like the Sustainable Livelihood Framework, play a crucial role in ensuring that development projects benefit communities equitably while minimizing adverse impacts. By focusing on livelihoods, cultural preservation, and equity, these frameworks guide decision-makers in creating inclusive and sustainable solutions. Despite challenges, their integration into impact assessment processes is essential for fostering holistic development

2.2 Principles of Impact Assessments

The principles of Impact Assessment ensure that the process is inclusive, scientifically robust, and geared toward sustainable outcomes. Key principles include:

a) Holistic Integration

Ensures the consideration of environmental, social, economic, and health impacts together.

Promotes a balanced approach, addressing trade-offs and synergies between different dimensions.

b) Proactive Planning

Emphasizes early identification and mitigation of risks, reducing costs and preventing irreversible damage.

c) Transparency and Accountability

Requires openness in methodologies, findings, and decision-making to build public trust and credibility.

d) Equity and Inclusivity

Ensures that marginalized and vulnerable groups are considered, and their voices are heard during the assessment process.

e) Evidence-Based Decision Making

Uses robust scientific data, stakeholder inputs, and empirical research to support conclusions and recommendations.

2.3 Stakeholder Theory and Public Participation

Stakeholder engagement is integral to IA, ensuring that diverse perspectives are included and potential conflicts are mitigated.

a) Understanding Stakeholder Theory

Definition: Stakeholder theory emphasizes the importance of involving all parties affected by a project, including communities, governments, NGOs, and private entities.

Importance: Stakeholders bring unique insights, concerns, and knowledge, which enhance the quality of the IA process.

b) Levels of Participation

- Inform: Providing stakeholders with clear, accessible information.
- Consult: Gathering feedback through surveys, focus groups, and public meetings.
- Involve: Actively engaging stakeholders in discussions and decision-making.
- Collaborate: Partnering with stakeholders to develop solutions.
- Empower: Allowing stakeholders to make decisions directly.

c) Benefits of Public Participation

- Enhances transparency and legitimacy.
- Reduces conflicts and delays caused by opposition.
- Ensures culturally and contextually relevant solutions.

d) Challenges in Stakeholder Engagement

- Managing conflicting interests.
- Ensuring participation of marginalized groups.
- Balancing transparency with confidentiality.

2.4 Sustainability and Development Goals (SDGs) in Impact Assessment

Impact Assessments are vital tools for advancing the 2030 Agenda for Sustainable Development and achieving the Sustainable Development Goals

(SDGs). They provide a structured approach to align projects with global sustainability priorities.

a) Role of IA in Advancing SDGs

• SDG 6 (Clean Water and Sanitation): IA ensures that water resource projects protect ecosystems and maintain access to clean water.

• SDG 13 (Climate Action): Evaluates greenhouse gas emissions and proposes climate-resilient solutions.

• SDG 15 (Life on Land): Protects terrestrial ecosystems and biodiversity through mitigation strategies.

b) Linking IA to Sustainability Dimensions

• Environmental Sustainability: Mitigates pollution, conserves resources, and protects biodiversity.

• Social Sustainability: Promotes social equity, cultural preservation, and community resilience.

• Economic Sustainability: Ensures cost-effective and long-term benefits while minimizing risks.

c) Tools for SDG Integration

• Sustainability Indicators: Metrics that align IA objectives with SDG targets.

• Scenario Analysis: Evaluating how different project alternatives contribute to SDG outcomes.

• Sustainability Appraisal: Comprehensive evaluation of project contributions to all dimensions of sustainability.

d) Examples of IA Supporting SDGs

• Renewable Energy Projects: Assessing impacts on energy access (SDG 7) and climate mitigation (SDG 13).

• Urban Development Projects: Balancing infrastructure growth with reduced inequalities (SDG 10) and sustainable cities (SDG 11).

• Agricultural Initiatives: Ensuring food security (SDG 2) while protecting land and water resources (SDG 15).

The theoretical foundations of Impact Assessment provide a comprehensive framework for evaluating and addressing the environmental, social, economic, and health implications of development projects. Conceptual frameworks like PSR and LCA structure the assessment process, while principles such as transparency, inclusivity, and evidence-based decision-making ensure its effectiveness. Stakeholder engagement is critical for fostering participation and legitimacy, and alignment with the SDGs highlights IA's role in promoting sustainable development. Together, these theoretical underpinnings strengthen the credibility, relevance, and impact of IA as a decision-making tool.

CHAPTER III

Approaches and Models in Impact Assessment

Impact assessment is a multidimensional process that requires diverse approaches and models to evaluate the outcomes of projects, policies, or programs. These approaches are designed to suit varying contexts, scales, and objectives, providing a comprehensive analysis of potential impacts. This chapter elaborates on key approaches and models in impact assessment, including their definitions, methodologies, applications, and limitations.

3.1 Quantitative vs. Qualitative Approaches

3.1.1 Quantitative Approaches in Impact Assessment

Quantitative approaches are central to impact assessment methodologies, particularly for projects and policies requiring measurable, objective data to analyze potential or realized outcomes. These approaches focus on the systematic collection, processing, and analysis of numerical data, making them highly reliable for drawing conclusions and informing decision-making.

3.1.2 Key Features of Quantitative Approaches

Quantitative approaches are defined by the following distinct characteristics:

I) Structured Data Collection Methods:

Data is collected using pre-designed instruments, such as structured surveys, experiments, censuses, and monitoring systems. These tools are essential for ensuring consistency and replicability.

For example, a government may use household surveys to assess the economic impacts of a newly implemented social welfare program.

II) Numerical Analysis:

Data collected is analyzed using statistical tools such as regression analysis, variance analysis (ANOVA), and hypothesis testing. Mathematical models, like econometric simulations, are also common.

For instance, time-series data can be analyzed to assess the long-term economic growth stimulated by an industrial development project.

III) Results Representation:

Findings are typically presented through visual aids, such as graphs, tables, and charts. Statistical indicators like mean, median, standard deviation, and confidence intervals are often highlighted.

An air quality assessment project might visualize data using bar charts to depict pollutant levels across different time periods.

3.1.3 Applications of Quantitative Approaches

Quantitative approaches are versatile and are applied across various domains in impact assessment:

I) Environmental Monitoring:

Quantitative methods are used to estimate pollution levels, assess biodiversity changes, and monitor resource depletion.

Example: Air or water quality indices (e.g., AQI or Biochemical Oxygen Demand) provide measurable indicators to evaluate environmental health in areas impacted by urbanization or industrial activities.

II) Economic Evaluations:

Methods such as cost-benefit analysis (CBA) and input-output modeling assess the financial implications of projects.

Example: Evaluating the return on investment (ROI) for renewable energy projects by comparing the long-term cost savings with initial capital expenditure.

III) Public Health Assessments:

Quantitative approaches measure the health impacts of policies, such as vaccination programs or clean water initiatives, using indicators like disease incidence or mortality rates.

Example: Analysis of hospital admission rates to evaluate the health benefits of reducing air pollution in metropolitan areas.

IV) Infrastructure Projects:

The impacts of large-scale infrastructure projects like highways, dams, and railways are assessed using transportation models and demographic data.

Example: Estimating traffic flow and reduction in travel time resulting from a new expressway.

3.1.4 Strengths of Quantitative Approaches

Quantitative approaches offer several advantages, making them indispensable for large-scale and data-driven impact assessments:

I) Objectivity and Replicability:

Quantitative data is less susceptible to biases, offering a high degree of objectivity. This is critical for projects where impartiality and scientific rigor are essential.

Replicability ensures that findings can be validated through repeated assessments under similar conditions.

II) Scalability:

These approaches are effective for large-scale studies involving extensive datasets. National or regional-level policies often rely on quantitative impact assessments for evaluation.

Example: Nationwide assessments of literacy rates post-implementation of education reforms.

III) Precision and Granularity:

Statistical analysis enables precise measurements and detailed insights, such as demographic variations or time-specific trends.

Example: Analyzing urban vs. rural differences in employment outcomes following industrial expansion.

IV) Decision Support:

Quantitative data supports evidence-based policymaking by providing clear metrics and benchmarks.

Example: Setting pollution control limits based on threshold values derived from quantitative studies.

3.1.5 Limitations of Quantitative Approaches

Despite their strengths, quantitative approaches have notable limitations:

I) Contextual Oversight:

These methods often fail to capture nuanced, subjective, or contextual information, such as community sentiments or cultural values.

Example: A quantitative assessment of economic growth may overlook the social cost of displaced communities.

II) Data-Intensive Requirements:

Quantitative methods require extensive data collection, which can be resource-intensive in terms of time, costs, and technical expertise.

Example: Installing real-time monitoring systems for water quality can be financially burdensome for low-income regions.

III) Complexity in Interpretation:

Misinterpretation of data can lead to flawed conclusions. It requires skilled professionals to analyze and derive accurate insights.

Example: Correlation between two variables (e.g., education levels and income) might be misinterpreted as causation without thorough analysis.

IV) Adaptability Issues:

Predefined frameworks and models may lack flexibility, particularly in dynamic or rapidly changing scenarios.

Example: An emergency response project might require adaptive assessments that quantitative models struggle to provide in real-time.

3.1.6 Illustrative Examples of Quantitative Approaches

I) Air Quality Monitoring:

A city government uses real-time air quality sensors to measure pollutant concentrations (e.g., PM2.5 and NO2). Statistical analysis reveals seasonal patterns, aiding the implementation of emission control policies during peak pollution periods.

II) Economic Growth Evaluation:

A rural development program aims to boost household incomes. Surveys conducted pre- and post-program implementation show a 25% increase in average income levels, validating the program's effectiveness.

III) Health Policy Analysis:

To assess the impact of a vaccination drive, statistical tools analyze disease incidence rates before and after implementation. Results indicate a significant decline in infection rates, supporting continued investment in immunization programs.

3.1.7 Quantitative Approaches in Practice

Quantitative methods have been instrumental in assessing large-scale projects and policies. For instance:

I) Case Study: Environmental Impact Assessment:

A coal mining project conducts a quantitative analysis of groundwater contamination using sampling and laboratory tests. Data reveals elevated heavy metal concentrations, prompting mitigation measures like water treatment systems.

II) Case Study: Social Infrastructure Development:

The construction of a metro rail system uses quantitative models to estimate travel time savings, reduced vehicular emissions, and economic productivity gains. These metrics justify public investment in the project.

Quantitative approaches are integral to impact assessment methodologies, providing objective, scalable, and precise insights into various aspects of projects and policies. However, their limitations highlight the importance of integrating complementary qualitative methods to ensure a holistic analysis. By leveraging the strengths of quantitative data and addressing its shortcomings, decision-makers can achieve more balanced and effective outcomes in impact assessment.

This comprehensive discussion underscores the significance of quantitative methods while acknowledging the need for context-sensitive adaptations in real-world applications.

3.1.8 Qualitative Approaches in Impact Assessment

Qualitative approaches are invaluable in impact assessments for exploring non-quantifiable aspects such as social, cultural, and behavioral dimensions. They provide a nuanced understanding of the lived experiences, perceptions, and values of individuals and communities affected by policies, programs, or projects.

I. Key Features of Qualitative Approaches

Qualitative approaches are characterized by their exploratory and interpretative nature:

I) Unstructured Methods:

Data is collected through flexible, open-ended methodologies that allow for in-depth exploration of complex issues.

Examples:

- Interviews: One-on-one conversations to gather personal insights or experiences.
- Focus Groups: Group discussions to explore shared perceptions and collective opinions.
- Case Studies: Detailed examination of specific instances or examples within a broader context.
- Prioritization of Subjective Understanding:

Emphasis is placed on interpreting the perceptions, values, and experiences of individuals or communities rather than numerical data.

For instance, understanding how women in a rural area perceive the impact of improved road connectivity on their livelihoods.

II) Contextual Sensitivity:

Qualitative approaches excel in capturing the nuances of local contexts, cultural settings, and unique circumstances that quantitative methods might overlook.

3.1.9 Applications of Qualitative Approaches

Qualitative methods are applied across diverse domains in impact assessment, including:

I) Social Equity Assessments:

Examining how urban development projects, such as housing or transportation, impact different demographic groups.

Example: Understanding the experiences of displaced communities due to large-scale infrastructure projects and identifying gaps in resettlement policies.

II) Cultural Impact Studies:

Exploring the implications of projects on cultural practices, traditions, and heritage.

Example: Assessing how the construction of a hydroelectric dam affects indigenous communities' cultural ties to ancestral lands.

III) Community Attitudes Toward Projects:

Investigating community responses to initiatives like renewable energy installations or waste management facilities.

Example: Using focus groups to explore residents' concerns about the installation of wind turbines in their locality.

IV) Health and Well-being:

Understanding the psychosocial impacts of projects on health and well-being, such as stress levels or community cohesion.

Example: Evaluating how the introduction of community healthcare centers affects marginalized populations' access to healthcare.

3.1.10 Strengths of Qualitative Approaches

I) In-depth Insights:

Qualitative methods provide a detailed, nuanced understanding of complex issues, often uncovering hidden factors influencing outcomes.

Example: An in-depth case study might reveal underlying social dynamics that contribute to the failure of a rural development project.

II) Flexibility:

These methods are highly adaptable to dynamic or changing contexts, making them suitable for exploratory research.

Example: Focus group discussions can be tailored based on participants' responses to delve deeper into emerging themes.

III) Rich Narratives:

Qualitative data can capture rich narratives, stories, and testimonies, offering a human-centered perspective to impact assessments.

Example: Documenting the voices of women affected by urban renewal projects can provide compelling evidence for advocacy.

IV) Empowering Marginalized Voices:

These approaches prioritize inclusivity, giving a platform to underrepresented or marginalized groups.

Example: Engaging with indigenous communities to understand the cultural significance of natural resources threatened by industrial projects.

3.1.11 Limitations of Qualitative Approaches

I) Subjectivity:

The interpretative nature of qualitative research introduces potential biases, as findings depend heavily on the researcher's perspective.

Example: A researcher's preconceived notions might influence how data from interviews is interpreted.

II) Generalizability:

Due to the focus on specific contexts, qualitative findings are often not generalizable to broader populations or situations.

Example: Insights from a focus group in one region may not apply to communities in different cultural or socio-economic settings.

III) Resource-Intensive:

Qualitative methods can be time-consuming and require skilled researchers to collect, analyze, and interpret data effectively.

Example: Conducting a series of ethnographic studies might demand significant time and expertise.

IV) Complex Data Analysis:

Analyzing qualitative data involves identifying patterns, themes, and narratives, which can be challenging and less straightforward than quantitative analysis.

Example: Coding and synthesizing data from hundreds of interview transcripts is a labor-intensive process.

3.1.12 Illustrative Examples of Qualitative Approaches

I) Social Equity in Urban Development:

A study on urban housing redevelopment explores the lived experiences of low-income families displaced by gentrification. Interviews reveal their struggles with higher rents, longer commutes, and loss of community networks.

II) Community Perspectives on Renewable Energy:

Focus groups in rural areas examine residents' perceptions of a new solar farm. Discussions highlight initial resistance due to lack of awareness, but also reveal opportunities for economic benefits once concerns are addressed.

III) Health Impacts of Environmental Pollution:

Case studies in industrial zones document how pollution affects local residents' health. Narratives from affected families provide a human face to statistical health data, emphasizing the urgency of interventions.

3.1.12 Steps in Conducting Qualitative Impact Assessments

I) Designing the Study:

Define the research questions and identify the target population.

Select appropriate qualitative methods, such as focus groups or ethnographic studies.

II) Data Collection:

- Conduct interviews, focus group discussions, or field observations.

- Use audio recordings, field notes, or video documentation to capture data.

III) Data Analysis:

- Transcribe and organize collected data.

Use thematic analysis or grounded theory to identify key patterns and themes.

IV) Reporting:

- Present findings using rich narratives, direct quotes, and case studies.

- Highlight implications for policy or project design.

3.2 Integrating Qualitative Approaches with Quantitative Methods

While qualitative approaches excel in exploring depth and context, combining them with quantitative methods provides a more comprehensive analysis. For example:

A mixed-methods study might use surveys (quantitative) to measure community satisfaction with a project and focus groups (qualitative) to explore the reasons behind the levels of satisfaction.

Qualitative approaches are indispensable in impact assessments for capturing the nuanced and human-centered dimensions of impacts. Their flexibility and depth make them particularly useful in understanding social, cultural, and behavioral aspects that are often overlooked by quantitative methods. However, their limitations in terms of subjectivity and generalizability underscore the importance of careful design and integration with quantitative techniques. By leveraging the strengths of qualitative research, impact assessments can provide richer, more actionable insights that drive more equitable and sustainable outcomes.

Comparison

The choice between quantitative and qualitative approaches depends on the objectives and nature of the assessment. Often, a combination of both methods is ideal for capturing a holistic perspective.

3.2.1 Mixed-Methods Approach in Impact Assessment

The mixed-methods approach integrates both quantitative and qualitative research methodologies to leverage the strengths of each. By combining the objectivity of quantitative data with the contextual richness of qualitative insights, mixed-methods research provides a more holistic understanding of complex issues in impact assessment. This approach is particularly effective in evaluating multi-dimensional impacts across environmental, social, economic, and cultural domains.

3.2.2 Understanding the Mixed-Methods Approach

I) Definition and Rationale

Mixed-methods research is an interdisciplinary approach that draws on both numerical and narrative data to address research questions. It seeks to: Cross-validate findings by comparing results from different methodologies. Address research questions that neither quantitative nor qualitative methods can fully answer independently.

Provide a richer and more nuanced understanding of impacts.

II) Methodology of the Mixed-Methods Approach

The mixed-methods approach is typically implemented using one of three primary designs:

1. Sequential Design

In this design, one method informs or complements the other in a phased manner:

• Qualitative-to-Quantitative:

Qualitative research (e.g., focus groups) identifies key themes or variables, which are then measured quantitatively (e.g., through surveys).

Example: Conducting interviews to understand community perceptions of water quality issues, followed by a survey to quantify the prevalence of concerns.

• Quantitative-to-Qualitative:

Quantitative data highlights trends or anomalies that qualitative research can explore in depth.

Example: Analyzing air pollution indices to identify hotspots, then conducting community discussions to understand the social implications.

2. Concurrent Design

Both quantitative and qualitative methods are applied simultaneously, with findings integrated during the analysis phase.

Example: While conducting surveys to measure agricultural productivity, researchers simultaneously interview farmers to understand challenges in adopting new technologies.

3. Transformative Design

Focused on addressing specific equity or justice issues, such as gender disparities or marginalized community impacts.

Example: A gender analysis combines statistical data on women's workforce participation (quantitative) with interviews on barriers to employment (qualitative).

3.2.3 Applications of the Mixed-Methods Approach

The mixed-methods approach is versatile and widely applicable in various domains of impact assessment:

1. Health Impact Assessments (HIA)

• Quantitative Component: Measuring disease prevalence, mortality rates, or healthcare access.

• Qualitative Component: Exploring patient experiences, cultural attitudes towards healthcare, or barriers to treatment.

• Example: Analyzing the spread of a waterborne disease through epidemiological data (quantitative) and understanding community hygiene practices through focus groups (qualitative).

2. Education Program Evaluations

• Quantitative Component: Tracking enrollment rates, attendance, and academic performance.

• Qualitative Component: Collecting teacher feedback, student narratives, or parental opinions.

• Example: Assessing the success of a rural education program by measuring literacy rates and conducting interviews with students and teachers.

3. Environmental Impact Assessments (EIA)

• Quantitative Component: Monitoring pollutant levels or biodiversity indices.

• Qualitative Component: Understanding local community perceptions of environmental changes.

• Example: Analyzing deforestation rates (quantitative) alongside interviews with indigenous populations to explore cultural impacts.

4. Social Equity and Gender Assessments

• Quantitative Component: Measuring gender wage gaps or employment statistics.

• Qualitative Component: Documenting women's experiences in the workforce.

• Example: Evaluating a women's entrepreneurship program by combining business growth metrics with participant testimonials.

3.3.3 Strengths of the Mixed-Methods Approach

I) Comprehensive Understanding:

Mixed methods capture both the breadth and depth of impacts.

Example: Measuring the economic benefits of a road project quantitatively (e.g., increased trade) while exploring social impacts (e.g., improved access to education) qualitatively.

II) Validation and Cross-Checking:

Results from one method can validate or complement findings from the other, reducing biases.

Example: If survey data suggests high satisfaction with a project, qualitative interviews can confirm or challenge these findings.

III) Flexibility:

The approach can be adapted to suit various research contexts and questions.

Example: A climate resilience study might combine quantitative modeling of rainfall patterns with qualitative accounts from farmers.

IV) Policy Relevance:

The mixed-methods approach provides actionable insights by addressing both measurable outcomes and human experiences.

Example: Policymakers can use quantitative data to set targets and qualitative insights to design interventions.

3.3.4 Challenges of the Mixed-Methods Approach

I) Resource-Intensive:

Conducting mixed-methods research requires significant time, budget, and personnel.

Example: A large-scale housing project might involve extensive surveys and multiple focus groups across diverse communities.

II) Technical Expertise:

Researchers must be proficient in both quantitative and qualitative methodologies.

Example: Expertise is required to integrate statistical analysis with thematic coding of interviews.

III) Complex Data Integration:

Combining datasets with different formats and scales can be challenging.

Example: Merging survey results with narrative interview data requires careful methodological alignment.

IV) Ethical Considerations:

Balancing confidentiality and data-sharing across methodologies is crucial.

Example: Quantitative health data may require anonymization, while qualitative interviews necessitate informed consent.

3.3.5 Illustrative Examples of Mixed-Methods Research

Example 1: Rural Electrification Project

• Objective: Evaluate the impacts of electrification on rural households.

• Quantitative Findings: Increased household income by 20% due to extended working hours.

• Qualitative Insights: Women reported improved quality of life due to reduced reliance on kerosene lamps.

Example 2: Urban Transportation Initiative

• Objective: Assess the social and environmental impacts of a new metro system.

• Quantitative Findings: Reduction in traffic congestion by 30%.

• Qualitative Insights: Commuters expressed satisfaction with reduced travel times but highlighted concerns about high fares.

3.3.6 Steps to Conduct Mixed-Methods Research

I) Define Research Objectives:

Clearly articulate the goals and research questions to align methodologies.

II) Design the Study:

Select the appropriate mixed-methods design (sequential, concurrent, or transformative).

III) Data Collection:

- Use surveys, experiments, or censuses for quantitative data.

- Conduct interviews, focus groups, or ethnographic studies for qualitative data.

IV) Data Integration:

- Merge findings during analysis, ensuring consistency and coherence.

V) Reporting:

- Present results using a combination of statistical indicators, graphs, and narrative accounts.

The mixed-methods approach is a powerful tool in impact assessment, offering a comprehensive understanding of multi-faceted issues. By integrating numerical precision with human-centered narratives, it enables researchers to uncover deeper insights, validate findings, and inform more effective policies and interventions. While resource-intensive and methodologically complex, its ability to address the limitations of single-method approaches makes it an indispensable strategy in modern research and impact evaluation.

3.4 Logical Framework Approach (LFA)

The Logical Framework Approach (LFA) is a project management and planning tool that organizes objectives, activities, outputs, and outcomes in a systematic and structured manner. Widely adopted in development initiatives funded by organizations such as the Asian Development Bank

(ADB), United Nations Development Programme (UNDP), and the World Bank, the LFA offers a clear framework for designing, monitoring, and evaluating projects. This chapter explores the components, methodology, applications, strengths, and limitations of the Logical Framework Approach.

3.4.1 Overview of the Logical Framework Approach

Definition

LFA is a methodology for:

Planning: Identifying the goals, purpose, and outputs of a project.

Implementation: Systematically executing planned activities to achieve objectives.

Evaluation: Assessing whether the intended outcomes and impacts have been realized.

Purpose

The LFA ensures that all stakeholders share a common understanding of project objectives, key activities, and the relationships between inputs, outputs, and desired impacts. By aligning efforts, it improves project efficiency and accountability.

3.4.2 Components of the Logical Framework Approach

I) Goal

- Represents the long-term impact or overall aim of the project.

- Example: Improve rural livelihoods through better road connectivity.

II) Purpose

- Refers to the immediate objectives or changes expected as a result of the project.

- Example: Enhance accessibility to markets, schools, and healthcare facilities in rural areas.

III) Outputs

- Tangible, measurable results directly produced by project activities.

- Example: Constructed roads, operational water supply systems, or trained personnel.

IV) Activities

- Actions undertaken to produce outputs.

- Example: Conducting surveys, procuring materials, or training workers.

3.4.3 Steps in the Logical Framework Approach

I) Problem Identification

- Identify and analyze the core issues that the project seeks to address.

- Tools: Problem trees, stakeholder consultations, and situational analyses.

- Example: Inadequate road infrastructure leading to poor market access and economic stagnation.

II) Objective Analysis

- Transform identified problems into objectives using an "objective tree."

- Example: Addressing "poor road connectivity" as an objective to "enhance rural transportation infrastructure."

III) Logical Framework Matrix Development

- The logical framework matrix (logframe) serves as a concise representation of project elements. It includes:

• Narrative Summary: Outlines goals, purposes, outputs, and activities.

• Objectively Verifiable Indicators (OVIs): Specifies measurable criteria to evaluate success.

• Means of Verification (MoV): Identifies sources of data for each indicator.

• Assumptions/Risks: Lists external factors critical to achieving success.

• Applications of the Logical Framework Approach

I. Infrastructure Development Projects

• Road Construction: LFA helps in defining objectives such as reducing travel time, improving market accessibility, and enhancing regional connectivity.

• Water Supply Systems: Projects use the LFA to ensure water quality, availability, and equitable distribution.

II. Social Development Initiatives

• Education: Used to design programs that aim to increase literacy rates or enhance school infrastructure.

• Health: Applied to initiatives targeting disease control, healthcare accessibility, or public health awareness.

III. Environmental Projects

• Applied to programs focused on conservation, renewable energy deployment, or pollution control.

• Example: A reforestation project might use LFA to plan activities, track planted areas, and measure ecological restoration.

IV. Donor-Funded Projects

• Organizations like ADB, UNDP, or the World Bank rely on the LFA for structured planning and reporting.

• Example: Monitoring the impact of rural electrification programs on local communities.

3.4.4 Strengths of the Logical Framework Approach

I. Clarity and Structure

LFA simplifies complex projects into manageable components, ensuring clarity among stakeholders.

Example: In a multi-phase road construction project, LFA clearly delineates short-term outputs (constructed roads) and long-term goals (economic growth).

II. Facilitates Communication

Promotes dialogue between project planners, implementers, and beneficiaries by providing a shared understanding of objectives and processes.

Example: A water management project might use LFA to align government agencies, contractors, and community groups.

III. Focus on Results

Emphasizes measurable outcomes, ensuring accountability and continuous improvement.

Example: A health program tracks disease reduction using predefined indicators.

IV. Versatility

Applicable to diverse sectors, including infrastructure, education, health, and environment.

Example: LFA is equally effective in planning a rural electrification project or a school modernization initiative.

3.4.5 Limitations of the Logical Framework Approach

I. Oversimplification of Complex Issues

- By focusing on predefined objectives, LFA may not fully capture the complexities or evolving nature of certain projects.

- Example: Social equity issues in urban development might require adaptive, context-sensitive approaches.

II. Rigidity in Planning

- The linear nature of LFA limits adaptability to unforeseen challenges or changing circumstances.

- Example: A disaster relief project might struggle to incorporate unexpected changes in community needs.

III. Resource-Intensive Development

- Developing a comprehensive logframe requires significant time, expertise, and stakeholder input.

- Example: Extensive consultations for a national climate resilience program.

IV. Risk of Neglecting External Factors

- Over-reliance on assumptions may lead to underestimating external risks.

- Example: Political instability disrupting project implementation.

3.4.6 Illustrative Example: Applying LFA to a Rural Road Connectivity Project

I. Problem Identification

Core Issue: Lack of road infrastructure hampers economic opportunities and access to services.

II. Objective Analysis

Objective: Construct all-weather roads to connect rural communities with markets, schools, and healthcare facilities.

III. Logical Framework Matrix

Narrative Summary Objectively Verifiable Indicators (OVIs) Means of Verification (MoV) Assumptions/Risks

Goal: Improve rural livelihoods 10% increase in household income by 2028 Household surveys Stable economic conditions

Purpose: Enhance accessibility 50% reduction in travel time to key facilities Transport surveys Timely completion of roads

Outputs: Construct 100 km of roads 100 km of paved roads by 2025 Project completion reports Availability of funds

Activities: Conduct surveys, procure materials, and build roads - Activity logs -

The Logical Framework Approach (LFA) is a powerful tool for planning and managing projects across sectors. Its structured methodology enables clear goal-setting, efficient resource allocation, and effective monitoring and evaluation. However, its success depends on careful implementation, stakeholder engagement, and the ability to adapt to changing circumstances. By addressing its limitations, LFA can continue to serve as an indispensable methodology in the field of development and impact assessment.

3.5 Theory of Change (ToC) Model

3.5.1 The Theory of Change (ToC) Model: A Comprehensive Overview

The Theory of Change (ToC) model is a framework used to conceptualize, design, and evaluate the processes through which projects or programs achieve desired results. Unlike traditional models that may focus solely on outputs or activities, ToC emphasizes the interconnected pathways that link inputs, activities, outputs, outcomes, and impacts. This comprehensive approach facilitates strategic planning, robust monitoring, and evidence-based evaluation.

3.5.2 Key Elements of the Theory of Change Model

I) Inputs

- Inputs refer to the foundational resources required for a project. These can include financial resources, human capital, infrastructure, materials, or technological tools.
- Examples: Funding from donors, skilled personnel, office equipment, and community partnerships.
- Significance: Inputs provide the starting point for implementing activities and ensuring the project's viability.

II) Activities
- Activities are the interventions or actions undertaken to achieve the project's objectives. These activities are designed based on the desired outputs and outcomes.
- Examples: Conducting training programs, building infrastructure, or organizing awareness campaigns.
- Significance: Well-planned activities lay the foundation for producing meaningful outputs.

III) Outputs
- Outputs represent the immediate, tangible results of the activities. They are the first measurable indicators of progress within a project.
- Examples: Number of schools built, workshops conducted, or policies drafted.
- Significance: Outputs act as the bridge between activities and outcomes.
-

IV) Outcomes
- Outcomes are the medium-term changes or results that occur as a direct result of the outputs. These changes can be behavioral, institutional, or systemic.
- Examples: Improved literacy rates, enhanced community engagement, or increased adoption of renewable energy practices.
- Significance: Outcomes provide evidence of progress toward achieving the project's long-term goals.

V) Impacts
- Impacts are the broader, long-term effects that result from the cumulative influence of outcomes. These impacts align with overarching societal goals such as poverty alleviation, environmental sustainability, or gender equity.
- Examples: Reduced poverty levels, sustainable development, or enhanced gender parity.
- Significance: Impacts highlight the ultimate success and relevance of a project in addressing critical challenges.

3.5.3 Applications of the Theory of Change Model

The ToC model is widely applied in various domains to design, implement, and evaluate programs.

I. Social Impact Assessments

- Mapping Development Pathways: ToC is used to visualize how specific interventions (e.g., vocational training programs) lead to enhanced employment opportunities and improved community welfare.

- Example: A women's empowerment initiative might use ToC to link skill-building workshops (activities) with increased income levels (outcomes) and gender equality (impacts).

II. Monitoring and Evaluation Frameworks

- Tracking Progress: ToC helps in establishing performance indicators at different stages—outputs, outcomes, and impacts—to monitor the effectiveness of interventions.

- Example: In a public health project, ToC could link vaccination campaigns (activities) to reduced disease prevalence (outcomes) and improved life expectancy (impacts).

III. Policy and Program Design

- Strategic Planning: Policymakers use ToC to identify the steps needed to achieve long-term societal goals.

- Example: A government might design a rural electrification program, linking activities (installation of solar panels) to outcomes (increased energy access) and impacts (economic growth and improved quality of life).

IV. Disaster Management and Resilience Building

- Framework for Action: ToC can outline pathways for recovery and resilience, linking disaster relief activities to long-term community rehabilitation.

- Example: Distribution of relief materials (outputs) leads to enhanced preparedness (outcomes) and reduced vulnerability to future disasters (impacts).

3.5.4 Strengths of the Theory of Change Model

I. Visual Representation of Processes

- ToC employs diagrams and flowcharts to illustrate the relationships between inputs, activities, outputs, outcomes, and impacts.

- Benefit: Simplifies complex projects for stakeholders, enhancing communication and understanding.

- Example: A renewable energy project might depict how investing in solar technology (inputs) results in reduced carbon emissions (impacts).

II. Encourages Adaptive Management

- ToC allows for flexibility in responding to emerging challenges or opportunities during project implementation.

- Benefit: Facilitates course correction to ensure that objectives remain achievable.

- Example: Adjusting community engagement strategies in a conservation project based on feedback from initial outreach efforts.

III. Focuses on Accountability and Evidence

- By defining clear pathways and performance indicators, ToC ensures accountability to stakeholders.

- Benefit: Builds credibility and fosters trust among donors, partners, and beneficiaries.

- Example: A microfinance program might use ToC to demonstrate how loans (activities) lead to business growth (outcomes) and poverty reduction (impacts).

IV. Applicable Across Sectors

- ToC is versatile and can be adapted to diverse fields such as education, healthcare, environment, and governance.

- Benefit: Promotes cross-sectoral learning and innovation.

- Example: Combining health and education initiatives to address malnutrition and improve academic performance.

3.5.5 Limitations of the Theory of Change Model

I. Requires Continuous Monitoring

- ToC demands regular data collection and analysis to track progress and validate assumptions.

- Challenge: Resource-intensive, requiring skilled personnel and advanced tools.

- Example: In a rural water supply project, ongoing monitoring of water quality and user satisfaction may strain limited resources.

II. Subject to Interpretation Biases

- Stakeholders may have differing perspectives on the cause-and-effect relationships depicted in ToC.

- Challenge: Risk of misalignment or conflicting priorities.

- Example: Disagreement among stakeholders about whether improved transport access directly leads to economic growth.

III. Complexity in Multisectoral Projects

- Mapping pathways for projects involving multiple sectors or stakeholders

can be challenging.
- Challenge: Difficulty in capturing interdependencies and unintended consequences.
- Example: A climate adaptation project integrating agriculture, water management, and infrastructure development.
IV. Focus on Predefined Objectives
- ToC prioritizes planned outcomes, potentially overlooking emergent or unintended results.
- Challenge: Limited adaptability to evolving circumstances.
- Example: A literacy program might neglect broader societal impacts such as increased civic engagement.

3.5.6 Example of ToC in Practice

I. Case Study: Education for All Initiative
Goal: Achieve universal primary education.
Inputs: Funding, trained teachers, school infrastructure.
Activities: Teacher training, curriculum development, enrollment drives.
Outputs: Increased enrollment, improved classroom facilities.
Outcomes: Enhanced literacy rates, reduced dropout rates.
Impacts: Socioeconomic empowerment, reduced poverty, and enhanced quality of life.

The Theory of Change model is a powerful tool for understanding and navigating the pathways through which projects achieve their desired impacts. By emphasizing causal linkages and adaptive management, ToC enhances strategic planning, monitoring, and evaluation. However, its effectiveness hinges on the availability of resources, stakeholder collaboration, and the ability to address its inherent challenges. With thoughtful implementation, ToC can drive transformative change and sustainable development across diverse sectors.

3.6 Cost-Benefit Analysis (CBA)

Cost-Benefit Analysis (CBA) is a decision-support tool used to evaluate the economic efficiency of projects or policies by systematically comparing their costs and benefits in monetary terms. CBA is widely employed in various sectors, including infrastructure, energy, healthcare, and education, to determine whether the benefits of a proposed project outweigh its costs and to identify the most economically viable options among alternatives.

3.6.1 Key Components of Cost-Benefit Analysis

I. Costs
- Costs refer to the resources required to implement a project, including

direct and indirect expenses. These can be further categorized as:

- Capital Costs: Initial investments, such as construction expenses, equipment purchases, or land acquisition.
- Operating Costs: Recurring expenses like maintenance, labor, and utilities.
- Opportunity Costs: The benefits foregone by choosing one option over others.
- External Costs: Negative externalities, such as environmental degradation or social disruption.

II. Benefits

- Benefits are the positive outcomes or value generated by the project. These can include:
- Direct Benefits: Tangible results, such as increased revenue or reduced travel time.
- Indirect Benefits: Spillover effects, like enhanced economic activity in the region.
- Non-Monetary Benefits: Improvements in quality of life, health, or environmental sustainability.

III. Monetization

- The process of quantifying and expressing both costs and benefits in monetary terms. While direct costs and benefits are often straightforward to monetize, indirect and intangible factors (e.g., environmental or social impacts) require proxies or valuation methods, such as willingness-to-pay surveys.

IV. Discounting

- Future costs and benefits are adjusted to their present value using a discount rate, accounting for the time value of money.

V. Net Present Value (NPV): The difference between discounted benefits and costs.

VI. Benefit-Cost Ratio (BCR): The ratio of total discounted benefits to costs.

3.6.2 Steps in Conducting Cost-Benefit Analysis

Step 1: Identify Costs and Benefits

Clearly outline all potential costs and benefits associated with the project. Include direct, indirect, tangible, intangible, and external factors.

Example: In a highway construction project, costs might include construction materials and land acquisition, while benefits could be reduced travel time and fuel savings.

Step 2: Quantify and Monetize Costs and Benefits

Use market prices, expert assessments, or econometric models to assign monetary values.

For intangible factors, employ methods like contingent valuation or hedonic pricing.

Example: The economic value of reduced air pollution can be estimated using health cost savings.

Step 3: Discount Future Values

Apply a suitable discount rate to calculate the present value of future costs and benefits.

Example: A 5% discount rate might be used to evaluate the long-term benefits of renewable energy projects.

Step 4: Calculate Key Metrics

Compute NPV, BCR, and internal rate of return (IRR).

Example: A project with an NPV of $10 million and a BCR of 2.5 is considered highly viable.

Step 5: Sensitivity Analysis

Test the robustness of results by varying key assumptions, such as discount rates or cost estimates.

Example: Assess how changes in fuel prices affect the viability of a public transport project.

Step 6: Decision-Making

Use CBA results to inform policy decisions, prioritize projects, or allocate resources.

Example: Choose between two energy projects based on their respective BCRs.

3.6.3 Applications of Cost-Benefit Analysis

I. Infrastructure Projects

- CBA is widely used to evaluate the economic feasibility of infrastructure investments.

- Example: Assessing the benefits of a new bridge by calculating time savings, reduced vehicle operating costs, and increased economic connectivity.

II. Energy Projects

- In the energy sector, CBA helps compare options like fossil fuels, renewable energy, and energy efficiency programs.

- Example: A solar farm project may have higher initial costs but yield long-term savings and environmental benefits, making it favorable in a CBA.

III. Environmental Policies

- CBA is essential for assessing the economic implications of environmental regulations and conservation initiatives.

- Example: Evaluating the cost of air pollution controls against the health and productivity benefits they generate.

IV. Healthcare

- Healthcare projects often use CBA to weigh treatment costs against health benefits.

- Example: Vaccination programs are analyzed for their cost savings from avoided medical treatments and productivity losses.

V. Education and Social Programs

- CBA helps determine the return on investment in education and social welfare projects.

- Example: Analyzing how early childhood education programs impact long-term earnings and social mobility.

3.6.4 Strengths of Cost-Benefit Analysis

I. Objective Decision-Making

- CBA provides a quantitative basis for evaluating projects, reducing subjective biases.

- Example: Comparing highway expansion and public transit investments based on NPV.

II. Prioritization of Resources

- By quantifying returns, CBA helps allocate resources to projects with the highest economic efficiency.

- Example: Choosing among renewable energy projects based on their respective BCRs.

III. Policy Justification

- CBA aids in demonstrating the economic rationale behind public policies or investments.

- Example: Justifying subsidies for electric vehicles by highlighting long-term environmental benefits.

IV. Comprehensive Evaluation

- Incorporates direct, indirect, and external factors, offering a holistic view of project impacts.

- Example: Including ecosystem services in the valuation of forest conservation projects.

3.6.5 Limitations of Cost-Benefit Analysis

I. Challenges in Monetizing Intangibles

- Some benefits, like cultural heritage or biodiversity, are difficult to express in monetary terms.

- Example: Valuing the social significance of a historic landmark.

II. Equity Concerns

- CBA often prioritizes efficiency over equity, potentially marginalizing disadvantaged groups.
- Example: A highway project might benefit urban commuters but displace rural communities.

III. Uncertainty in Estimates

- Projections of costs and benefits are subject to uncertainty, especially in long-term projects.
- Example: Predicting the economic impact of climate change mitigation measures.

IV. Dependence on Discount Rate

- The choice of discount rate significantly influences outcomes, often favoring short-term benefits over long-term sustainability.
- Example: High discount rates may undervalue future benefits of renewable energy.

V. Static Framework

- CBA assumes linear relationships, which may not capture the dynamic and interconnected nature of complex systems.
- Example: Overlooking indirect benefits of education on community health.

3.6.5 Cost-Benefit Case Study:

I. Renewable Energy Project

• Scenario: A government is considering a large-scale solar farm to reduce dependence on fossil fuels.

• Costs:

- Capital investment: $500 million.
- Operational and maintenance costs: $20 million/year.
- Benefits:
- Reduced greenhouse gas emissions: $50 million/year.
- Energy savings: $100 million/year.
- Health benefits from improved air quality: $30 million/year.
- Results:
- NPV: $1.2 billion (assuming a 5% discount rate).
- BCR: 2.4 (for every dollar spent, $2.40 is gained).
- Decision: The project is economically viable and environmentally beneficial.

Cost-Benefit Analysis is a critical tool for evaluating the economic viability of projects and policies. Its strengths lie in its objectivity, quantitative rigor, and ability to prioritize resources. However, it must be applied with caution, particularly when dealing with intangible benefits, equity concerns, and uncertainties. By combining CBA with complementary approaches like Multi-Criteria Analysis (MCA), decision-makers can achieve more balanced and inclusive evaluations.

3.7 Multi-Criteria Analysis (MCA)

I. Overview:

- Considers multiple criteria, both quantitative and qualitative, to evaluate project alternatives.
- Uses scoring and weighting systems for decision-making.

II. Steps:

- Define criteria and indicators.
- Assign weights to criteria.
- Score and rank alternatives.

III. Applications:

- Environmental assessments comparing energy generation methods.
- Urban development projects prioritizing green spaces.

IV. Strengths:

- Flexible and adaptable.
- Incorporates stakeholder preferences.

V. Limitations:

- Subjective weighting and scoring.
- Results depend on chosen criteria.

3.7.1 Multi-Criteria Analysis (MCA): A Comprehensive Exploration

Multi-Criteria Analysis (MCA) is a robust decision-making framework that evaluates projects or policies by considering multiple criteria, which can be both quantitative and qualitative. Unlike single-dimensional analyses like Cost-Benefit Analysis (CBA), MCA accommodates diverse factors such as economic, environmental, social, and technical aspects, providing a comprehensive evaluation of alternatives. It is especially useful in complex scenarios where trade-offs between conflicting objectives must be assessed

3.7.2 Key Components of Multi-Criteria Analysis

I. Criteria and Indicators

- Criteria: Broad parameters or dimensions used to evaluate alternatives (e.g., cost, environmental impact, social equity).
- Indicators: Specific metrics or proxies that quantify or describe the performance of alternatives against each criterion (e.g., CO_2 emissions per

unit energy for environmental impact).

II. Scoring System

- Each alternative is evaluated and assigned a score based on its performance against each criterion. Scoring methods can include:
- Numeric scales (e.g., 1 to 10).
- Qualitative descriptors (e.g., high, medium, low).

III. Weighting

- Weights are assigned to each criterion to reflect its relative importance in the decision-making process. Stakeholder preferences, policy priorities, or expert opinions often guide this step.

IV. Aggregation

- The weighted scores across all criteria are aggregated to determine the overall performance of each alternative. This step helps rank the alternatives.

3.7.3 Steps in Conducting Multi-Criteria Analysis

Step 1: Define Criteria and Indicators

- Identify the relevant criteria for evaluation based on project objectives and stakeholder inputs.
- Choose indicators that effectively measure each criterion.
- Example: For an energy project, criteria might include cost, environmental impact, and social acceptance. Indicators could include investment cost, CO_2 emissions, and public support.

Step 2: Assign Weights to Criteria

- Determine the relative importance of each criterion using:
- Expert consultations.
- Stakeholder engagement.
- Analytic Hierarchy Process (AHP) or similar techniques.
- Example: In a renewable energy project, environmental impact might receive a higher weight than cost, reflecting policy priorities on sustainability.

Step 3: Score Alternatives

- Evaluate each alternative against the defined indicators and assign scores.
- Use methods such as:
- Direct scoring (e.g., assigning values based on expert judgment).
- Empirical data analysis (e.g., emission levels or cost comparisons).
- Example: Solar energy might score high on environmental impact but lower on cost compared to natural gas.

Step 4: Rank Alternatives

- Aggregate the weighted scores to calculate the overall performance of each alternative.
- Rank the alternatives to identify the most preferred option.
- Example: A project with a higher aggregate score indicating better alignment with criteria might be ranked first.

3.7.4 Applications of Multi-Criteria Analysis

I. Environmental Assessments

- MCA is widely used in environmental impact evaluations, particularly for comparing alternatives in energy generation, waste management, and resource conservation.
- Example: Comparing coal, solar, wind, and nuclear energy generation methods based on criteria like cost, emissions, land use, and public acceptance.

II. Urban Development

- Urban planners use MCA to prioritize projects or policies that enhance liveability, sustainability, and inclusivity.
- Example: Evaluating urban development proposals based on green space allocation, transportation access, and economic benefits.

III. Transportation Planning

- MCA helps optimize transportation projects by balancing cost-efficiency, environmental sustainability, and social equity.
- Example: Choosing between expanding a highway, building a new public transit line, or enhancing bike paths.

IV. Water Resource Management

- In water projects, MCA supports decisions about allocation, infrastructure investments, and conservation strategies.
- Example: Ranking water treatment technologies based on criteria like cost, efficiency, and environmental impact.

V. Policy Analysis

- Policymakers use MCA to evaluate regulatory or investment options, ensuring alignment with diverse societal goals.
- Example: Assessing the impact of carbon pricing policies on economic growth, emissions reduction, and social equity.

3.7.5 Strengths of Multi-Criteria Analysis

I. Flexibility and Adaptability

- Accommodates both quantitative and qualitative data.
- Can be customized for various sectors and decision-making contexts.
- Example: In urban planning, MCA can integrate traffic data (quantitative)

and community feedback (qualitative).

II. Stakeholder Engagement

- Encourages stakeholder participation, enhancing the legitimacy and acceptability of decisions.
- Example: Assigning weights to criteria based on consultations with affected communities.

III. Comprehensive Evaluation

- Considers diverse dimensions of impact, addressing trade-offs between conflicting objectives.
- Example: Balancing economic development with environmental conservation in infrastructure projects.

IV. Supports Transparent Decisions

- Provides a clear framework for documenting assumptions, scores, and weights, fostering transparency.
- Example: Publishing the weighting and scoring process in public project evaluations.

3.7.6 Limitations of Multi-Criteria Analysis

I. Subjectivity in Weighting and Scoring

- Weighting and scoring processes can introduce biases, influencing results.
- Example: Overemphasizing cost in a renewable energy evaluation might undervalue long-term environmental benefits.

II. Dependency on Chosen Criteria

- Results are sensitive to the selection of criteria, which might omit critical factors.
- Example: Ignoring social equity in urban development might favor economically efficient but socially inequitable options.

III. Resource-Intensive

- Requires extensive data collection, stakeholder engagement, and expert input.
- Example: Conducting MCA for a large infrastructure project might demand significant time and financial resources.

IV. Complexity in Interpretation

- Aggregated scores may oversimplify complex trade-offs, making it harder to justify decisions.
- Example: High aggregate scores for a controversial project might not resonate with affected stakeholders.

3.7.7 Case Study: Renewable Energy Policy Evaluation

Scenario: A government must choose between wind, solar, and natural gas as energy generation options.

Criteria and Weights:

• Environmental Impact (40%).

• Cost (30%).

• Social Acceptance (30%).

Scoring:

• Wind: 8 (environmental), 7 (cost), 6 (social acceptance).

• Solar: 9 (environmental), 6 (cost), 7 (social acceptance).

• Natural Gas: 5 (environmental), 8 (cost), 8 (social acceptance).

Results:

• Wind: 7.2 (weighted score).

• Solar: 7.4 (weighted score).

• Natural Gas: 6.8 (weighted score).

Decision: Solar energy is the preferred option, balancing sustainability and social acceptance effectively.

Multi-Criteria Analysis is an invaluable tool for decision-makers navigating complex projects or policies involving diverse impacts. By integrating quantitative and qualitative dimensions, MCA ensures a holistic evaluation that aligns with stakeholder priorities and broader societal goals. While it requires careful attention to biases and resource demands, its flexibility and comprehensiveness make it a vital approach in sustainable development, infrastructure planning, and policy formulation.

3.8 Conclusion

Impact assessment is a critical process used to evaluate the effects of projects, policies, or programs on various stakeholders, environments, and economies. It involves understanding and measuring the changes brought about by an intervention, whether positive, negative, or neutral, and is often a key component of project planning, monitoring, and evaluation. Over time, numerous approaches and models have been developed to guide this evaluation process, each offering a unique perspective or methodology to analyze and interpret the results of the intervention. These methods can be broadly classified into quantitative, qualitative, and mixed-methods approaches, each with its strengths and limitations.

The quantitative approach to impact assessment is grounded in data and numerical analysis. This approach typically involves collecting and analyzing statistical data to assess the scale and nature of the impact, often through surveys, experiments, or secondary data sources. The key strength of quantitative methods is their ability to provide objective, measurable, and replicable results. They can be used to assess the effectiveness of an intervention with a high degree of precision, such as measuring changes in income, health outcomes, or educational attainment. Methods like Cost-Benefit Analysis (CBA) and Multicriteria Analysis (MCA) rely heavily on quantitative data to compare the costs and benefits of a project or to evaluate the performance of different options based on predefined criteria. However, the quantitative approach also has limitations. It can often oversimplify complex social, cultural, and environmental dynamics, failing to capture the full breadth of a project's impact. Additionally, the reliance on data collection can be resource-intensive, requiring significant time, money, and effort to ensure the accuracy and reliability of the data. Furthermore, quantitative methods may not adequately account for the subjective experiences and perspectives of stakeholders, which can be crucial in understanding the real impact of a project, especially in terms of social and cultural outcomes.

On the other hand, qualitative approaches emphasize understanding the deeper, often subjective, impacts of a project. This method involves collecting non-numerical data through interviews, focus groups, case studies, or ethnographic research, providing insights into the experiences, perceptions, and narratives of those affected by the intervention. Qualitative methods are particularly effective at capturing the nuances of human behavior and social dynamics, making them useful for exploring complex or intangible outcomes, such as changes in community cohesion, empowerment, or cultural identity.

The strength of qualitative methods lies in their ability to uncover insights that quantitative methods may miss. They can provide rich, contextualized data that allows evaluators to understand how and why a project has affected its beneficiaries. For example, qualitative assessments of women's empowerment programs may reveal changes in self-confidence, access to decision-making processes, or shifts in gender norms, all of which may not be easily quantified. Qualitative approaches also allow for flexibility and adaptability, as the research design can evolve based on emerging findings.

However, qualitative methods also have their challenges. They tend to be more subjective, making it difficult to generalize results across larger populations. The interpretation of qualitative data can vary depending on the evaluator's perspective, and the findings may not always be replicable. Moreover, qualitative research can be time-consuming and labor-intensive, especially when gathering and analyzing data from diverse sources.

Additionally, the findings may lack the precision that quantitative methods can provide, which may limit their usefulness for decision-making in certain contexts.

To address the limitations of both approaches, mixed-methods approaches have emerged as a more holistic approach to impact assessment. Mixed methods combine both quantitative and qualitative data collection and analysis techniques, allowing evaluators to leverage the strengths of each approach while compensating for their respective weaknesses. By triangulating data from different sources and methodologies, mixed-methods approaches provide a more comprehensive understanding of a project's impact. For instance, a project that seeks to improve health outcomes might use quantitative surveys to measure changes in health indicators while also conducting qualitative interviews to explore the personal stories of patients, healthcare providers, and community members.

The mixed-methods approach is particularly useful when assessing complex, multi-dimensional projects that involve diverse stakeholders. It allows for the integration of numerical data with contextual insights, offering a richer, more nuanced evaluation. This approach also enhances the validity of the findings by cross-checking results across different data sources and methods. However, the main drawback of mixed methods is that they require expertise in both quantitative and qualitative research techniques, making the design and implementation more complex. Moreover, the integration of different types of data can be challenging, and there may be conflicts between the results of the different methods that need to be resolved.

In addition to these general approaches, several specific frameworks and methodologies can be applied to impact assessment. The Logical Framework Approach (LFA) and Theory of Change (ToC) are two widely used frameworks that provide structured pathways for planning, implementing, and evaluating projects. Both LFA and ToC are designed to clarify the logical connections between inputs, activities, outputs, outcomes, and impacts, ensuring that the project's objectives are clearly defined and measurable. These frameworks help evaluators identify key assumptions, risks, and assumptions, ensuring that all elements of the project are aligned towards achieving the intended results.

LFA is particularly useful for projects with clearly defined, measurable goals and a well-established cause-and-effect relationship. It provides a systematic way to track progress and identify deviations from the planned outcomes. On the other hand, the Theory of Change framework is more flexible and focused on understanding the underlying assumptions and pathways that lead to change. It is particularly useful for complex, long-term projects where the path to impact is not linear and where a deeper understanding of the change process is needed.

Cost-Benefit Analysis (CBA) and Multicriteria Analysis (MCA) are other important methods in impact assessment, providing decision-making tools that help evaluate the relative value of different project options. CBA is a quantitative approach that compares the costs and benefits of a project, determining whether the benefits outweigh the costs. It is particularly useful for assessing the financial viability of a project and comparing alternatives. MCA, on the other hand, evaluates projects based on multiple criteria, which may include social, environmental, and economic factors. It is a more flexible approach, suitable for projects with multiple, often conflicting, objectives.

The selection of the appropriate impact assessment model depends on several factors, including the project's objectives, context, and stakeholder needs. In some cases, a simple quantitative analysis may suffice, especially for projects with clear, measurable outcomes. In other instances, a more nuanced qualitative or mixed-methods approach may be required to capture the full range of impacts. Similarly, frameworks like LFA and ToC provide structured pathways for ensuring project goals are aligned with desired outcomes, while decision-making tools like CBA and MCA offer valuable insights into the financial and social trade-offs involved.

Ultimately, the goal of any impact assessment is to ensure that projects are effectively evaluated, that lessons are learned, and that future interventions can be improved based on evidence. By selecting the appropriate impact assessment model, evaluators can provide stakeholders with the information needed to make informed decisions, enhance accountability, and promote the long-term sustainability of projects.

CHAPTER IV

Key Steps in Impact Assessment

Impact assessment is a systematic process used to evaluate the potential effects of a project, policy, or program before it is implemented. This process is essential for identifying, understanding, and mitigating negative impacts while enhancing positive outcomes. Effective impact assessment involves several critical steps that guide the evaluation from the initial project idea to the final report. These steps include screening and scoping, baseline data collection and analysis, impact identification and prediction, mitigation and enhancement measures, evaluation and monitoring plans, and reporting and review. Each of these stages plays a vital role in ensuring the comprehensive and accurate assessment of a project's impact.

4.1 Screening and Scoping

Screening and scoping are the critical initial steps in the impact assessment process that play a vital role in shaping the overall direction and scope of the assessment. These two phases help establish whether an impact assessment (IA) is necessary and define the extent and boundaries of the assessment itself. Screening determines the need for an impact assessment, while scoping ensures that the assessment focuses on the most relevant and significant aspects of the project. Together, they form the foundation for a comprehensive and efficient impact assessment, setting the tone for the subsequent stages of the process.

Screening: Determining the Need for Impact Assessment

Screening is the first stage of the impact assessment process. Its primary objective is to determine whether a proposed project or development requires a full-scale impact assessment. This initial step serves as a filtering process, helping identify projects that may have significant environmental, social, or economic consequences and, therefore, need detailed evaluation. Screening is crucial because it prevents unnecessary or irrelevant assessments, saving both time and resources.

4.1.1 Purpose of Screening

The purpose of screening is to evaluate whether a project or activity is likely to have significant effects, and if so, whether these effects require further analysis through a formal impact assessment. Many types of projects, particularly large infrastructure developments or those that may affect sensitive ecosystems, communities, or public health, have the potential for significant impacts. Screening helps identify these projects early in the process, ensuring that a full impact assessment is conducted when necessary.

A project that is likely to have significant impacts on the environment, economy, or society may need to undergo a detailed environmental and social impact assessment (ESIA) to ensure that any adverse effects are minimized and mitigated. On the other hand, smaller or less impactful projects may not require a full assessment. By screening out projects that are unlikely to have significant impacts, resources can be focused on those that have the greatest potential to cause harm or benefit.

4.1.2 Screening Process

The screening process typically involves the following key components:

Project Characteristics: The nature and characteristics of the proposed project are examined to determine whether it is likely to have significant environmental, social, or economic effects. Projects that involve large-scale land use changes, resource extraction, or industrial development, for example, are more likely to require a full impact assessment.

Location and Setting: The geographical location of the project plays a crucial role in determining the potential for significant impacts. Projects located in sensitive areas—such as wetlands, coastal zones, or protected natural reserves—are more likely to require detailed assessments due to their proximity to vulnerable ecosystems. Similarly, projects near residential areas, schools, or cultural sites may have social implications that need to be carefully considered.

Threshold Criteria: Many jurisdictions establish threshold criteria that outline the types of projects or activities that are subject to screening. These criteria may be based on project size (e.g., the area of land affected, the volume of resources extracted), project type (e.g., energy, transportation, industrial), or potential risks (e.g., hazardous materials, emissions). For instance, a mining project may require an assessment based on its size, while a smaller-scale community facility may not.

Past Project Experiences: The screening process may also involve reviewing similar projects in the region or elsewhere to assess the likely environmental and social impacts. For example, if similar projects have caused significant deforestation, air pollution, or social disruption in the past, it may trigger the need for a full impact assessment for the proposed project.

Legal and Regulatory Requirements: In many jurisdictions, screening is a mandatory requirement for certain types of projects. For example, the European Union's Environmental Impact Assessment Directive and various national regulations stipulate that certain projects automatically require an assessment. Local government authorities or regulatory agencies often provide guidelines for screening to ensure that projects comply with environmental laws and regulations.

The output of the screening process is typically a decision on whether a project requires a full-scale environmental and social impact assessment (ESIA) or a more simplified review (such as a scoping study). In some cases, projects may be exempted from further assessment if the potential impacts are deemed negligible or well-understood.

4.1.2 Scoping: Defining the Boundaries of the Impact Assessment

Once it has been determined that a full impact assessment is necessary, the next step is scoping. Scoping defines the scope and boundaries of the impact assessment by identifying the specific environmental, social, and economic factors that need to be evaluated, the stakeholders who should be involved, and the methodologies to be used. This phase is crucial for ensuring that the impact assessment is focused on the most significant issues and that all relevant concerns are addressed.

4.1.3 Purpose of Scoping

The purpose of scoping is to narrow the focus of the impact assessment to the most important issues, allowing for a more efficient and relevant evaluation. Scoping ensures that the impact assessment does not become an overwhelming or unfocused exercise by clearly defining the areas to be studied, the stakeholders to be engaged, and the potential impacts to be analyzed. This step helps to avoid "scope creep," where unnecessary issues are introduced, leading to unnecessary costs and delays.

Scoping also provides an opportunity for stakeholders, including local communities, experts, and relevant authorities, to provide input into the assessment. By identifying key issues early in the process, scoping helps ensure that the perspectives of affected parties are considered in the evaluation.

4.1.4 Scoping Process

Scoping involves several critical activities:

Defining the Project Boundaries: One of the first steps in scoping is to define the geographical boundaries of the impact assessment. This includes not only the immediate area of the project but also the surrounding region that may be affected by the project. For example, a dam project may have far-reaching impacts on downstream communities, wildlife habitats, and water quality, all of which need to be considered in the scope of the assessment.

Identifying Key Environmental, Social, and Economic Issues: Scoping involves identifying the potential impacts that should be considered in the impact assessment. This may include environmental factors such as air and water quality, biodiversity, and soil degradation, as well as social issues such as health risks, displacement, and community well-being. Economic impacts such as job creation, income distribution, and local business development are also considered.

Stakeholder Engagement: Scoping involves identifying key stakeholders and determining the best methods for engaging them in the process. Stakeholders may include local communities, government agencies, non-governmental organizations (NGOs), and experts in relevant fields. Effective stakeholder engagement is critical for understanding local concerns, gathering relevant data, and ensuring that the impact assessment reflects the views of all those who may be affected by the project.

Setting the Assessment Criteria: The scoping process establishes the criteria against which the potential impacts will be assessed. This includes deciding how impacts will be measured (e.g., through quantitative data, qualitative assessments, or expert judgment), determining the significance thresholds (i.e., the level of impact that will be considered significant), and defining the indicators that will be used to evaluate the impacts.

Selecting Methods and Tools for Data Collection: During scoping, the methods and tools that will be used to collect data and analyze the impacts are determined. This may include field surveys, interviews with stakeholders, modeling techniques, and review of secondary data. The choice of methods depends on the specific impacts being studied and the resources available for data collection.

Setting the Time Frame: Scoping helps establish the time frame for the impact assessment. This includes determining how long the assessment will take, when baseline data will be collected, and the timing of consultations and reviews with stakeholders. The time frame also determines the specific phases of the project that need to be covered in the assessment (e.g., construction, operation, and decommissioning).

Identifying Mitigation Measures: Scoping includes an initial review of possible mitigation measures for identified impacts. This helps to guide the development of the full assessment by identifying areas where mitigation strategies will be necessary. For example, if a project threatens water quality, scoping may suggest the inclusion of water treatment measures as part of the impact assessment.

4.1.5 The Role of Stakeholders in Scoping

Stakeholder involvement is a crucial aspect of the scoping process. Early engagement with local communities, affected parties, and relevant experts ensures that the assessment process reflects the concerns of those most likely to be impacted by the project. Stakeholders may provide valuable information on local environmental conditions, social issues, and economic needs, which can help shape the focus of the impact assessment.

Effective stakeholder engagement during scoping also helps build trust and transparency between project developers and local communities. By involving stakeholders early in the process, project proponents can identify potential conflicts and address concerns before they escalate into major issues.

4.1.6 Outputs of Screening and Scoping

The outputs of screening and scoping are essential for guiding the rest of the impact assessment process. The outcome of the screening phase is typically a decision about whether a full impact assessment is required. If the project is deemed to have potential significant impacts, the scoping phase defines the focus areas for the detailed assessment.

The scoping phase produces key documents, such as the scoping report, which outlines the geographic boundaries of the assessment, the key impacts to be studied, the stakeholders involved, the methods for data collection, and the overall timeline. These outputs guide the subsequent stages of the impact assessment, ensuring that the focus remains on the most critical issues.

In conclusion, screening and scoping are integral to the impact assessment process, ensuring that the right projects are assessed and that the assessment focuses on the most significant impacts. Screening serves as the first filter, determining which projects require detailed evaluation while scoping defines the boundaries of the assessment and ensures that the process remains focused and relevant. Both steps play a crucial role.

4.2 Baseline Data Collection and Analysis

Baseline data collection and analysis form a cornerstone of the impact assessment process. Once the scope of the assessment is determined through screening and scoping, the next critical step is to gather baseline data. Baseline data is essentially the pre-project condition of the environment, society, and economy. It provides a reference point against which the impacts and changes caused by the proposed project will be assessed. The accuracy and comprehensiveness of baseline data are crucial because they serve as the foundation for all future assessments, including impact prediction, mitigation strategies, and monitoring of post-project effects.

In this chapter, we will explore the importance of baseline data, the methods used for its collection, and the analytical techniques employed to interpret the data. This understanding is essential for ensuring the success of the impact assessment process and, ultimately, for managing the potential impacts of a project in a sustainable and informed manner.

4.2.1 Importance of Baseline Data

The significance of baseline data cannot be overstated. It serves several vital functions in the impact assessment process:

Establishing a Reference Point: Baseline data provides the pre-project conditions of the environment, society, and economy, creating a benchmark against which the potential effects of the project will be compared. Without this reference, it would be impossible to determine the extent of the impacts or whether they are significant enough to require mitigation.

Evaluating the Severity and Significance of Impacts: By understanding the existing conditions, the assessment can identify how the project might alter the landscape. Baseline data is essential for predicting the magnitude of changes, helping to prioritize which impacts require more attention and detailed analysis.

Guiding Decision-Making: The collection and analysis of baseline data enable project developers and decision-makers to understand the current status of key variables in the project area. This knowledge helps in shaping the project design, determining where mitigation measures are necessary, and making informed choices that minimize adverse impacts.

Tracking Progress and Effectiveness: Baseline data allows for effective monitoring and evaluation during the implementation phase and after the project's completion. By comparing post-project conditions with the baseline, it is possible to evaluate the effectiveness of mitigation measures and overall project performance.

Informing Stakeholders and Local Communities: Baseline data provides transparency in the decision-making process. Sharing this data with stakeholders, including local communities and affected populations, ensures they are aware of the existing conditions and the potential changes that may occur due to the project.

Legal and Regulatory Compliance: In many cases, baseline data collection is required by law or regulatory frameworks. Projects, particularly those with environmental or social impacts, often need to comply with specific standards, regulations, or environmental protection laws that mandate the collection of baseline data as part of the assessment process.

4.2.2 Types of Baseline Data

Baseline data encompasses a wide array of environmental, social, and economic variables. The following are the primary categories of data that are typically collected:

Environmental Data

Environmental baseline data is essential for understanding the ecological context of the proposed project and predicting the potential environmental impacts. This data typically includes:

Air Quality: The concentration of pollutants such as particulate matter (PM), nitrogen oxides (NOx), sulfur dioxide (SO2), carbon monoxide (CO), and volatile organic compounds (VOCs). This information is critical for assessing the air pollution impacts of the project.

Water Quality: Data on the chemical and physical properties of water sources, including parameters such as pH, turbidity, dissolved oxygen, temperature, and concentrations of specific contaminants like heavy metals, pesticides, and nutrients. Water quality data helps assess the impacts on local water resources, including rivers, lakes, groundwater, and coastal areas.

Soil Conditions: Data on soil types, fertility, contamination, erosion rates, and soil structure. This information is essential for understanding the effects of the project on agricultural productivity, land use changes, and erosion risks.

Vegetation and Biodiversity: Information on existing flora and fauna in the project area, including species diversity, abundance, and habitat quality. Biodiversity assessments help predict the project's impact on ecosystems and endangered species.

Climate and Weather Data: Local climate data, including temperature, precipitation, wind patterns, and seasonal variations, helps assess how the project might influence or be influenced by climate factors.

Noise Levels: Baseline data on ambient noise levels is essential for predicting the noise impacts of construction or operational activities. High noise levels can lead to significant social and health impacts.

Social Data

Social baseline data is essential to understand the local population, their living conditions, and how the project may affect them. Social data typically includes:

Demographic Information: Data on the population size, age structure, gender distribution, ethnic composition, and migration patterns. This data helps assess the potential social impact on different demographic groups, such as marginalized populations or vulnerable groups.

Health Statistics: Information on the health conditions of the local population, including common diseases, mortality rates, and access to healthcare services. Health data is critical for predicting potential public health impacts from the project, such as the spread of infectious diseases, or the impacts of pollution.

Education Levels: Data on literacy rates, school enrollment, and access to education helps assess the potential impacts of the project on local education systems and children.

Housing and Living Standards: Baseline data on housing quality, infrastructure, access to clean water and sanitation, and electricity availability provides insights into the living conditions of the affected communities.

Cultural and Social Practices: Information on the cultural practices, religious beliefs, languages, and social dynamics of the local communities. This helps identify potential conflicts or changes to social norms due to the project.

Economic Data

Economic baseline data is crucial for understanding the economic context of the project area. This data typically includes:

Employment Rates and Income Levels: Data on employment patterns, income distribution, and local sources of income. This data helps evaluate how the project might influence local employment opportunities, wage levels, and economic stability.

Local Economy and Livelihoods: Information on the key economic sectors, such as agriculture, fishing, industry, or services, which may be impacted by the project. Understanding local economic activities is important for assessing the economic risks and opportunities associated with the project.

Infrastructure and Utilities: Baseline data on the availability and quality of infrastructure, such as roads, transportation networks, telecommunications, and energy supply. This data helps assess the project's **potential to improve or disrupt infrastructure services in the area.**

4.2.3 Methods of Data Collection

The methods used for baseline data collection depend on the nature of the data, the geographical area, and the available resources. Common methods include:

Field Surveys

Field surveys are one of the most direct and reliable methods for collecting baseline data, particularly for environmental variables. Surveys involve direct observation, measurements, and sampling in the project area. Examples include water sampling for quality analysis, vegetation surveys, and noise level measurements. Field surveys can provide real-time data and are particularly useful for assessing current conditions in specific locations.

Remote Sensing

Remote sensing uses satellite imagery, drones, or aerial photography to gather large-scale environmental data. This method is particularly valuable for assessing changes in land use, vegetation cover, and hydrological conditions over time. Remote sensing is also useful in collecting data from areas that may be difficult to access on the ground.

Existing Records and Secondary Data

Secondary data includes existing government reports, academic studies, research papers, and environmental records that provide historical data on environmental, social, and economic conditions. Existing records are useful for establishing long-term trends and understanding the broader context in which the project will be implemented.

Stakeholder Interviews and Consultations

Interviews with local communities, government officials, and experts can provide valuable qualitative data that may not be captured through quantitative surveys. Stakeholder consultations help gather insights into local concerns, values, and knowledge that can enrich the baseline understanding of the project area. These consultations are particularly useful for understanding social dynamics, local livelihoods, and cultural practices.

4.2.4 Data Analysis and Interpretation

Once the baseline data has been collected, it is analyzed to interpret the current state of the environment, society, and economy. This analysis serves as the foundation for understanding how the project might affect these conditions. The data analysis typically involves:

Descriptive Statistics: Basic descriptive statistics are used to summarize and present the data. For example, calculating averages, ranges, and percentages for various environmental and social indicators.

Trend Analysis: Analyzing historical data to identify trends and patterns that can provide context for future changes. For example, examining long-term climate trends or economic growth patterns.

Geospatial Analysis: Geographic information system (GIS) tools are often used to analyze spatial data, such as land use patterns, vegetation cover, and the proximity of sensitive habitats to the project area.

Comparison and Benchmarking: The baseline data may be compared against established benchmarks or national and international standards. For example, comparing local air quality levels with air quality standards set by environmental authorities.

Baseline data collection and analysis are fundamental components of the impact assessment process. They provide a clear understanding of the pre-project conditions of the environment, society, and economy, enabling accurate predictions of potential impacts. The quality and accuracy of baseline data directly influence the effectiveness of the impact assessment and the subsequent development of mitigation strategies. By gathering a comprehensive set of data, from environmental indicators to social and economic conditions, the project team can ensure that the impact assessment is well-informed and able to address the most significant potential impacts.

4.3 Impact Identification and Prediction

Impact identification and prediction are crucial steps in the impact assessment process that follow the collection and analysis of baseline data. These steps involve determining how the project will interact with various environmental, social, and economic elements, and forecasting the potential positive and negative effects that may arise as a result. The goal is to systematically evaluate the direct and indirect impacts of the proposed project in order to understand its full range of potential consequences. This process helps in making informed decisions about whether the project should proceed, what mitigation measures are needed, and how to manage these impacts effectively.

In this chapter, we will elaborate on the process of impact identification and prediction, discussing how to systematically consider potential impacts, the methods and tools used for predicting those impacts, and the challenges associated with these tasks.

4.3.1 The Importance of Impact Identification and Prediction

Identifying and predicting impacts is central to the impact assessment process for several reasons:

Informed Decision Making: Impact identification provides the essential information needed to evaluate whether a project should proceed, be modified, or be abandoned. By understanding the potential consequences of a project, decision-makers can better determine whether the benefits outweigh the negative impacts or if alternative actions are necessary.

Resource Allocation: Proper identification and prediction of impacts help prioritize the allocation of resources for mitigation, monitoring, and management. Projects that are likely to have significant impacts may require additional resources for environmental protection, social support, and mitigation strategies.

Public and Stakeholder Engagement: Early identification of potential impacts facilitates transparency and engagement with stakeholders. It provides communities, local governments, and other concerned parties with the information necessary to assess the potential risks and benefits of the project and participate in the decision-making process.

Regulatory Compliance: Many countries and jurisdictions require an environmental or social impact assessment for certain types of projects. Accurate impact identification and prediction are necessary to ensure compliance with environmental laws and regulations and to avoid legal challenges or delays during project implementation.

Long-Term Sustainability: Impact identification and prediction help ensure the long-term sustainability of a project by addressing potential environmental, social, and economic risks. By anticipating negative impacts, strategies can be developed to avoid or minimize harm, while positive impacts can be enhanced to create long-term benefits.

4.3.2 Methods of Impact Identification

Impact identification is a systematic process that involves identifying both direct and indirect impacts of a project. The goal is to ensure that all potential effects are considered in the assessment. Several methods are used to facilitate this identification process:

Brainstorming and Expert Judgment

Brainstorming and expert judgment are key tools in impact identification. These methods involve gathering a team of subject matter experts who are familiar with the project and its context. This team can include environmental scientists, social scientists, engineers, and other relevant professionals who can provide insights into the potential consequences of the project. Brainstorming sessions allow for the generation of a wide range of potential impacts, which can then be refined through expert judgment to prioritize the most significant ones.

Experts often draw on their experience with similar projects or use available data to predict how the project will interact with the surrounding environment. They also assess historical data, case studies, and lessons learned from previous projects to inform the process.

Stakeholder Consultations

Stakeholder input is a critical component of impact identification. Local communities, indigenous groups, government agencies, non-governmental organizations (NGOs), and other stakeholders often have valuable knowledge and insights regarding the local environment, social structures, and potential risks. Involving stakeholders through consultations, workshops, focus groups, or interviews ensures that their concerns are taken into account and that the impacts that matter most to the people affected are properly identified.

Stakeholder consultations can also highlight indirect and long-term impacts that may not be immediately apparent to project planners and experts. For instance, a road construction project may result in changes to local trade routes, thereby influencing the local economy in unforeseen ways. Stakeholders may help identify these impacts early in the process.

Checklists and Impact Matrices

Checklists and impact matrices are structured tools that help ensure all potential impacts are systematically considered. These tools typically contain predefined lists of impact categories (e.g., air quality, water resources, social equity, cultural heritage) that can be marked off as relevant to the project. They may also include specific indicators or questions that guide the identification process.

Impact matrices can be used to link project activities with specific environmental, social, or economic impacts. For example, the matrix may outline how each stage of the project (e.g., construction, operation, decommissioning) may impact various resources (e.g., soil, water, air quality) and communities.

Scoping Reports

Scoping reports, which are often produced in earlier stages of the impact assessment process, provide a framework for impact identification. They outline the key issues, geographical scope, and methodologies for impact assessment. Scoping reports often focus on key areas of concern, such as biodiversity or water quality, and provide guidance on how to identify the most significant impacts within those areas.

The scoping process also helps set the boundaries for the impact assessment, highlighting which impacts should be given more detailed consideration and which can be excluded from the analysis. This ensures that resources are focused on the most important areas of potential impact.

4.3.3 Methods of Impact Prediction

Once impacts are identified, the next step is to predict their extent and significance. This step involves forecasting the potential changes in the environment, society, and economy as a result of the project. The methods of impact prediction can be broadly classified into qualitative assessments, quantitative models, and a combination of both.

Qualitative Assessment

Qualitative assessment is often used when predicting impacts that are difficult to quantify or when data is insufficient for precise modelling. In qualitative assessments, experts use their professional judgment and experience to predict the potential outcomes of a project. This approach often involves assessing the severity of impacts based on expert opinion, historical knowledge, and stakeholder consultations.

Qualitative assessments are particularly useful for predicting social and cultural impacts, where numerical data may not fully capture the nuances of community dynamics, health outcomes, or cultural disruptions. For example, a road construction project may result in increased traffic and noise, but the impact on local community cohesion or cultural heritage may be best predicted through qualitative assessments.

Quantitative Models

Quantitative models are used when data is available and when the impacts can be represented in numerical terms. These models are particularly useful for predicting environmental impacts such as air quality, water pollution, noise levels, and land use changes. For example, air pollution can be predicted using dispersion models that simulate how pollutants will travel through the atmosphere based on local weather conditions, emission sources, and topography.

Similarly, hydrological models can be used to predict the impact of a project on local water bodies, estimating changes in water quality or quantity due to construction activities, waste discharge, or changes in land cover. Quantitative models can also be applied to social and economic impacts, such as predicting changes in employment rates or economic output based on input-output models or demographic forecasting tools.

Combined Qualitative and Quantitative Methods

In many cases, a combination of qualitative and quantitative methods is used to provide a more comprehensive prediction of impacts. For instance, while a quantitative model may predict the air quality impact of a construction project, a qualitative assessment may be needed to predict how local communities will perceive these changes and how they will affect public health or community well-being.

For example, during a construction project, quantitative data may show that air quality levels will exceed regulatory limits. A qualitative assessment may then be conducted to predict the public health consequences, such as an increase in respiratory diseases or a rise in public complaints. Using both approaches allows for a more complete and nuanced understanding of potential impacts.

Sensitivity Analysis

Sensitivity analysis is a critical tool in impact prediction, especially when working with predictive models. It involves testing how changes in key assumptions or variables affect the predicted outcomes. Sensitivity analysis helps identify the most critical factors influencing the impacts and provides a range of potential outcomes, which accounts for uncertainty in the prediction process.

For example, in a model predicting water pollution, sensitivity analysis can be used to test how changes in precipitation, land use, or construction activities might affect the extent of pollution. By understanding the range of possible outcomes, decision-makers can better plan for the most likely impacts and identify the best mitigation strategies.

4.3.4 Challenges in Impact Identification and Prediction

Impact identification and prediction are inherently challenging processes due to various factors:

Uncertainty and Data Gaps: One of the biggest challenges is the uncertainty associated with predicting future conditions. Many impacts are difficult to predict with precision, especially for long-term and indirect effects. Data gaps, especially for new or poorly understood issues, can lead to incomplete or inaccurate predictions.

Complex Interactions: The interactions between different components of the environment, society, and economy are often complex and nonlinear.

Predicting the outcomes of these interactions can be difficult, especially when feedback loops or cumulative effects are involved.

Stakeholder Perspectives: Different stakeholders may perceive the impacts of the project differently. While one group may focus on environmental sustainability, another may prioritize economic growth. Balancing these perspectives and ensuring that all relevant impacts are identified and predicted can be challenging.

Political and Social Context: Political and social considerations may influence the identification and prediction of impacts. For example, certain impacts may be downplayed or overlooked due to political pressures or the interests of powerful stakeholders.

Impact identification and prediction are essential steps in the impact assessment process, as they provide the foundation for understanding the potential consequences of a project. By systematically identifying and forecasting the effects of a project, decision-makers can ensure that potential risks are managed, and opportunities are maximized. However, these processes are fraught with challenges, including uncertainty, data gaps, and complex interactions. By using a combination of qualitative and quantitative methods, conducting sensitivity analyses, and engaging stakeholders, the accuracy and reliability of impact prediction can be improved, ultimately leading to better project planning and management.

4.4 Mitigation and Enhancement Measures

Mitigation and enhancement measures are vital components of the impact assessment process, aimed at addressing the potential consequences of a project on the environment, society, and economy. After identifying and predicting the potential impacts of a project, the next logical step is to develop and implement strategies that reduce or eliminate negative impacts and maximize the positive ones. This chapter elaborates on the nature of mitigation and enhancement measures, their importance, types, and the processes involved in developing them.

4.4.1 The Importance of Mitigation and Enhancement Measures

Mitigation and enhancement measures are essential for several reasons:

Minimizing Adverse Impacts: The primary objective of mitigation measures is to minimize or avoid the adverse impacts of a project. Whether these impacts are environmental, social, or economic, mitigation strategies aim to prevent long-term harm, reduce risks, and ensure that negative effects do not outweigh the benefits of the project.

Enhancing Positive Outcomes: Enhancement measures aim to maximize the positive outcomes of a project. By promoting sustainability, improving local development, or fostering social equity, enhancement measures ensure that a project contributes positively to its surroundings, even as it meets its objectives.

Regulatory Compliance: Many countries and jurisdictions require the implementation of mitigation and enhancement measures as part of regulatory frameworks. For instance, the environmental impact assessment (EIA) process often mandates the identification of mitigation strategies, and failure to propose adequate measures can result in delays, additional scrutiny, or even project rejection.

Promoting Sustainable Development: Mitigation and enhancement measures are aligned with the principles of sustainable development. They support the achievement of long-term benefits without compromising the ability of future generations to meet their needs. By mitigating adverse effects and enhancing positive impacts, these measures help to ensure that development does not come at the cost of environmental degradation or social inequality.

Social License to Operate: Projects, particularly large-scale developments, must gain public acceptance. Effective mitigation of negative impacts, coupled with strategies to enhance positive ones, can help earn the social license to operate. This helps build trust among local communities and stakeholders, reducing opposition to the project and ensuring smoother implementation.

Managing Project Risks: Mitigation measures also serve to manage project risks by reducing the likelihood of unexpected or unintended consequences. By addressing potential issues before they arise, these measures help safeguard the project's reputation, financial stability, and long-term success.

4.4.2 Types of Mitigation Measures

Mitigation measures can take various forms, depending on the nature of the identified impacts and the project's context. These measures can be divided into different categories, including technical solutions, operational practices, social strategies, and policy interventions.Technical Solutions

Technical solutions focus on using advanced technologies and methods to minimize the environmental or social impacts of a project. These solutions are often the most direct and measurable form of mitigation. Examples of technical mitigation measures include:

Pollution Control Technologies: For projects that generate air, water, or noise pollution, installing pollution control devices can significantly reduce harmful emissions. Examples include scrubbers for air pollution, sediment control devices for water pollution, and sound barriers for noise reduction.

Waste Management Systems: Proper waste management systems, such as recycling, composting, and waste-to-energy technologies, can help mitigate the negative impacts of waste generated during the construction or operation of a project.

Sustainable Construction Practices: Employing sustainable construction techniques, such as using eco-friendly materials, reducing energy consumption, and minimizing waste during construction, can reduce the environmental footprint of a project. Examples include using low-carbon concrete, implementing energy-efficient building designs, or employing renewable energy sources during construction.

Energy Efficiency Measures: For projects that involve high energy consumption, energy efficiency measures, such as using low-energy machinery, optimizing energy usage, and incorporating renewable energy sources, can reduce the project's environmental impact.

Habitat Restoration and Protection: For projects that affect natural ecosystems, measures such as restoring degraded habitats, creating wildlife corridors, and protecting endangered species can help mitigate biodiversity loss.

Erosion Control: In areas prone to erosion, such as along riverbanks or on construction sites, mitigation measures can include the use of erosion control methods like silt fences, vegetation planting, and soil stabilization techniques to prevent soil degradation and sedimentation.

Operational Practices

Operational practices refer to the procedures and actions that can be implemented during the construction and operational phases of a project to minimize negative impacts. These measures may not involve technological solutions but instead focus on how the project is managed and executed. Examples include:

Adaptive Management Strategies: These strategies involve adjusting operations in response to unforeseen impacts. For example, if a project is found to be causing greater-than-expected environmental harm, operational changes can be made to reduce the impact.

Resource Efficiency Practices: Using fewer resources, including water, raw materials, and energy, during the project's operation can help mitigate environmental impacts. For instance, reducing the consumption of water and energy during the construction phase can lessen the demand on local resources.

Scheduling and Timing Adjustments: In projects where timing is critical (e.g., construction activities in sensitive ecosystems or wildlife habitats), adjusting the schedule to avoid critical seasons (e.g., breeding seasons for animals or wet seasons for plants) can help mitigate environmental disruption.

Noise and Vibration Control: Construction and operational activities that produce significant noise and vibration can be mitigated by scheduling high-impact activities during non-sensitive hours, using quieter machinery, and implementing noise reduction strategies.

Traffic Management: Construction projects often cause significant traffic disruptions. Mitigation measures include creating alternative routes, managing construction traffic, and scheduling work during off-peak hours to reduce traffic congestion and minimize social impacts.

Social and Organizational Strategies

Social and organizational strategies focus on managing the social impacts of a project. These measures are designed to address the human side of the project and may involve community engagement, compensation, and resettlement plans. Examples of social mitigation measures include:

Community Relocation and Compensation Programs: In cases where projects result in the displacement of local communities, mitigation measures may involve providing fair compensation, offering relocation assistance, and ensuring that displaced individuals or families are adequately supported.

Employment and Capacity Building Programs: Projects can mitigate negative social impacts by providing local employment opportunities, training, and capacity-building initiatives for affected communities. These programs help ensure that communities benefit economically from the project.

Public Health Initiatives: For projects that may affect public health, mitigation measures could include providing healthcare services, improving sanitation facilities, and establishing monitoring systems to track health-related impacts.

Cultural Preservation Programs: In cases where projects may affect local cultures or indigenous practices, mitigation measures can involve cultural preservation programs, such as safeguarding heritage sites or supporting community-driven cultural initiatives.

Community Development Initiatives: Projects can help mitigate negative social impacts by implementing community development initiatives that promote local economic development, infrastructure improvement, and social welfare. These may include building schools, health centers, or community centers, as well as supporting local businesses.

Policy Interventions and Legal Measures

In some cases, mitigation measures are implemented at the policy or legal level. These measures involve regulatory or contractual agreements to manage the project's impacts. Examples include:

Environmental Standards and Regulations: Projects may be required to comply with national or international environmental standards that set limits on pollution, waste disposal, and resource consumption. Legal frameworks can enforce these standards to ensure compliance.

Environmental Bonds or Insurance: For high-risk projects, companies may be required to post environmental bonds or obtain insurance that ensures the availability of funds for remediation in case of environmental damage.

Impact Monitoring and Auditing Requirements: Policy interventions may mandate ongoing monitoring of environmental or social impacts during the life of the project. Monitoring ensures that mitigation measures are implemented and that any unanticipated impacts are addressed promptly.

Environmental and Social Management Plans (ESMP): An ESMP is a formalized plan that outlines the strategies and actions required to mitigate impacts, monitor outcomes, and ensure that the project complies with legal and regulatory standards.

4.4.3 Types of Enhancement Measures

While mitigation measures focus on minimizing negative impacts, enhancement measures aim to maximize the positive effects of a project. These measures help ensure that a project contributes positively to the environment, society, and economy, providing additional benefits that extend beyond the project's immediate objectives.

Community Empowerment Initiatives

Enhancement measures often involve initiatives designed to improve the quality of life for local communities. These may include:

Skills Development and Training: By providing training programs for local workers, projects can enhance local employment opportunities and build capacity within the community.

Supporting Local Businesses: Initiatives that support local businesses through microcredit programs, training, and market linkages can foster economic growth and create sustainable livelihoods.

Access to Education and Health Services: Projects that invest in educational and healthcare infrastructure can help enhance social outcomes by improving access to essential services.

Environmental Sustainability Initiatives

Enhancement measures can also be aimed at promoting environmental sustainability. Examples include:

Sustainable Resource Management: Projects can implement sustainable practices for resource extraction, water management, and waste disposal, ensuring that natural resources are conserved for future generations.

Biodiversity Conservation: Initiatives aimed at protecting or enhancing local biodiversity, such as planting native species, creating wildlife corridors, and restoring damaged ecosystems, can improve environmental outcomes.

4.4.3.3 Economic Development Measures

Projects can include measures designed to boost local economies beyond the direct impacts of the project itself. These may include:

Infrastructure Development: Projects that include the development of infrastructure such as roads, schools, or public transport can enhance the overall quality of life in local communities.

Promotion of Sustainable Agriculture or Industry: By promoting sustainable agricultural practices or eco-friendly industries, projects can foster long-term economic growth that benefits local communities.

The development of mitigation and enhancement measures is a critical step in ensuring that a project achieves its objectives while minimizing harm and maximizing benefits. These measures should be based on the results of impact identification and prediction, be practical, cost-effective, and context-specific, and be supported by clear implementation plans. By adopting a comprehensive approach that includes both mitigation and enhancement measures, project planners and developers can enhance sustainability, improve social outcomes, and contribute to the long-term success of the project.

4.5 Evaluation and Monitoring Plans

Once mitigation and enhancement measures have been identified, it is essential to develop evaluation and monitoring plans to track the progress and effectiveness of these measures. Monitoring involves collecting data during the project's implementation and operation to ensure that the impacts are being managed as planned. Evaluation, on the other hand, assesses whether the project has achieved its intended objectives and whether the mitigation and enhancement measures have been effective in addressing the identified impacts.

Monitoring is an ongoing process that provides real-time data on the implementation of the project and its impacts. This data is used to track the effectiveness of mitigation and enhancement measures and to detect any unforeseen or unanticipated impacts. For example, monitoring may involve regular checks on air and water quality, social surveys to assess community satisfaction, or environmental audits to evaluate the success of conservation efforts.

Evaluation is typically conducted at specific points during the project, such as at the end of each phase or after the project has been fully implemented. The evaluation process compares the actual impacts of the project with the predicted impacts and assesses the success of mitigation and enhancement measures. It also provides feedback for future projects, helping to improve the design and implementation of future interventions.

4.6 Reporting and Review

The final step in the impact assessment process is reporting and review. This involves documenting the findings of the impact assessment, including the identification of potential impacts, the results of the baseline data analysis, the predicted impacts, and the proposed mitigation and enhancement measures. The report should provide a clear and transparent account of the assessment process, including the methods used, the data collected, and the conclusions drawn.

The review process allows stakeholders to provide feedback on the impact assessment, ensuring that all relevant issues have been addressed and that the findings are credible and reliable. This feedback is essential for ensuring that the project complies with legal and regulatory requirements and that the concerns of affected communities and other stakeholders are taken into account.

CHAPTER V

Impact assessment is a multifaceted process that requires the use of various tools and techniques to collect, analyze, and interpret data on potential project impacts. These tools help in ensuring that the assessment is comprehensive, accurate, and informed by empirical evidence. This chapter discusses the key tools and techniques commonly used in impact assessments, including data collection methods, geographic information systems (GIS) and remote sensing, statistical analysis and modeling tools, social and environmental indicators, and impact scoring and ranking techniques. These tools enable practitioners to assess, predict, and manage the impacts of development projects and interventions on the environment, society, and economy.

5.1 Data Collection Methods

The success of an impact assessment heavily depends on the quality and relevance of the data collected during the process. The first step is to select appropriate data collection methods that align with the project's objectives, scope, and the types of impacts being assessed. This section outlines some common methods used for collecting baseline and impact data: surveys and questionnaires, interviews and focus groups, and participatory rural appraisal (PRA).

5.1.1 Surveys and Questionnaires in Impact Assessment

Surveys and questionnaires are essential tools used to collect both quantitative and qualitative data in a wide range of social, environmental, and economic assessments. Their value lies in their ability to gather data from a large and diverse sample of stakeholders, often making them a go-to methodology for obtaining broad insights into the impacts of a project. Whether assessing a construction project, environmental policy change, or social program, surveys and questionnaires can provide critical information that drives decisions, evaluations, and strategies for mitigation and enhancement.

The Role of Surveys and Questionnaires in Impact Assessment

In an impact assessment, the goal is to forecast, understand, and address the potential impacts—both positive and negative—that a project may have on various stakeholders. Surveys and questionnaires provide a structured approach to gathering the required data, offering an efficient and standardized way to obtain information from a variety of respondents.

The data collected from surveys and questionnaires can contribute to:

Baseline Data Collection: Establishing the starting conditions before a project begins.

Impact Prediction: Understanding how the project is likely to affect different groups.

Monitoring and Evaluation: Tracking changes over time and determining the effectiveness of mitigation strategies or project interventions.

Public Consultation and Engagement: Understanding the concerns and perspectives of affected communities or stakeholders.

Guiding Decision-Making: Providing data that informs project design, implementation strategies, and adjustments based on findings.

Types of Surveys and Questionnaires

Surveys and questionnaires come in various forms, each serving different purposes. These types can be distinguished based on the scope of data collection (cross-sectional vs. longitudinal) and the structure of the questions (structured vs. semi-structured).

Cross-Sectional Surveys

Cross-sectional surveys are one of the most commonly used forms of data collection in impact assessments. A cross-sectional survey collects data at a single point in time from a sample of participants. The primary goal of this type of survey is to capture the current state or baseline conditions of a population, ecosystem, or environment.

Characteristics:

Provides a snapshot of the target group or environment at a particular moment.

Data is collected from a representative sample, ensuring that the findings are generalizable to the broader population.

The survey may include questions about demographics, attitudes, behaviors, or conditions that can be observed at the time of survey administration.

Quick and cost-effective in comparison to longitudinal studies.

Advantages:

Provides an efficient method for collecting data for baseline studies.

Useful for identifying key trends, issues, or concerns that may require attention during project implementation.

Facilitates comparisons between different groups, such as affected communities versus control groups.

Applications in Impact Assessment: Cross-sectional surveys are used in a variety of contexts. For example, in environmental impact assessments, a cross-sectional survey might be conducted to assess the current health of an ecosystem or community, focusing on factors such as biodiversity, air and water quality, or socio-economic conditions like income and education levels. This survey would then provide the baseline data necessary to compare the impacts that result from the project over time.

Longitudinal Surveys

In contrast to cross-sectional surveys, longitudinal surveys are conducted over a longer period of time, typically months or years. This type of survey is beneficial for monitoring changes that occur due to the implementation of a project or program.

Characteristics:

Data is collected from the same group of respondents at multiple points in time.

Allows researchers to track the evolution of various factors (e.g., social, economic, or environmental conditions) before, during, and after a project. Facilitates the examination of causal relationships by linking changes over time to the project's activities.

Advantages:

Provides insight into the temporal effects of a project.

Identifies trends and long-term changes that might not be immediately observable in cross-sectional data.

Helps to understand the sustainability of impacts over time.

Applications in Impact Assessment: Longitudinal surveys are particularly useful when assessing the long-term impacts of a project. For instance, in a project that aims to improve road infrastructure, a longitudinal survey might assess the changes in local community development, employment rates, and access to markets over several years. It would track how the infrastructure improvement translates into socio-economic benefits, such as reduced travel time, increased business opportunities, and better access to health and education services.

Structured Questionnaires

Structured questionnaires are a tool that uses a predefined set of closed-ended questions with a fixed set of response options. These questionnaires are designed to gather quantitative data that can be analyzed statistically. The structure of the questionnaire ensures that all respondents are asked the same questions in the same order, allowing for consistency and comparability across responses.

Characteristics:

Includes a fixed set of questions with predefined response categories (e.g., multiple choice, Likert scales).

Ideal for collecting data that can be quantified and analyzed using statistical methods.

Can be administered to a large number of respondents efficiently.

Advantages:

Easy to analyze due to standardized responses.

Allows for quick data collection from a large number of respondents.

Useful for identifying trends, patterns, and statistical correlations between variables.

Reliable for comparative analysis across different population groups.

Applications in Impact Assessment: In an environmental impact assessment, structured questionnaires can be used to assess the level of environmental awareness among local communities or to measure attitudes towards specific environmental policies. For example, a structured questionnaire could include questions on the community's perception of air quality, water contamination, or the effectiveness of mitigation measures. Responses can then be aggregated and analyzed to assess the general perception of the community regarding these issues.

Semi-Structured Questionnaires

Semi-structured questionnaires are more flexible than structured questionnaires because they combine both closed-ended and open-ended questions. While closed-ended questions help to capture quantitative data, open-ended questions allow respondents to provide detailed, qualitative responses.

Characteristics:

Includes both closed-ended and open-ended questions.

The interviewer has some flexibility to probe deeper into responses and ask follow-up questions.

Useful for obtaining a broader range of information, especially in terms of attitudes, perceptions, and experiences.

Advantages:

Offers a balance between quantitative and qualitative data.

Allows respondents to elaborate on their answers, providing a deeper understanding of their views and experiences.

Useful for gathering insights into complex or subjective issues that may not be captured by structured questions alone.

Applications in Impact Assessment: Semi-structured questionnaires are often used in social impact assessments to understand community members' attitudes towards a project. For example, in assessing the social impacts of a large development project, semi-structured questionnaires can include questions on local residents' concerns about displacement, changes in community dynamics, or perceptions of the benefits and risks associated with the project. The open-ended questions provide an opportunity for respondents to articulate concerns or ideas that may not be anticipated by the researchers.

Applications in Impact Assessment

Surveys and questionnaires can be used to collect a wide variety of data that is critical for understanding the potential impacts of a project. These tools can be applied across different sectors—social, economic, and environmental—to assess baseline conditions, monitor progress, and evaluate the effectiveness of mitigation measures. Below are specific examples of how surveys and questionnaires can be utilized in impact assessments:

Social Impact Assessment

In social impact assessments, surveys and questionnaires are used to gather data on how a project will affect local communities, including changes in social structures, cultural norms, and access to services. They can help identify potential disruptions to community life, changes in quality of life, and social cohesion.

Examples:

Assessing the community's awareness and perceptions of the project, such as concerns about displacement or resettlement.

Measuring the impact of the project on local employment opportunities, education, healthcare, and access to basic services.

Tracking changes in social capital, such as community engagement, participation in decision-making, and social networks.

Environmental Impact Assessment

In environmental impact assessments, surveys and questionnaires are typically used to evaluate baseline environmental conditions and gather community perceptions about environmental risks. They are particularly useful in projects that involve resource extraction, infrastructure development, or land use changes.

Examples:

Surveying local residents about their perceptions of environmental quality (e.g., air, water, noise pollution).

Collecting data on local biodiversity, land use, and ecosystem services that may be impacted by the project.

Gauging community attitudes toward mitigation measures, such as the establishment of wildlife corridors, pollution control measures, or environmental restoration efforts.

Economic Impact Assessment

Surveys and questionnaires are key tools in evaluating the economic impacts of a project, including changes in employment, income, economic growth, and local business development.

Examples:

Assessing how the project may create jobs, affect wages, or change the availability of skilled labor in the local economy.

Measuring the impact on local businesses, including changes in demand for goods and services, supply chain disruptions, or the creation of new market opportunities.

Evaluating the long-term economic benefits of the project, such as improvements in infrastructure, transportation, or access to markets.

Data Analysis and Reporting

The data collected through surveys and questionnaires require careful analysis and interpretation to derive meaningful insights for the impact assessment. Statistical techniques such as descriptive statistics, regression analysis, and factor analysis can be applied to process the data and identify trends, relationships, and key findings.

Descriptive Statistics: Summarizing the data through measures such as mean, median, mode, and standard deviation. This is useful for understanding the central tendency and variability of responses.

Inferential Statistics: Using statistical models to test hypotheses, make predictions, or determine causal relationships between variables.

Qualitative Analysis: Analyzing open-ended responses using methods like thematic analysis or content analysis to identify patterns and key themes.

Surveys and questionnaires are integral tools in impact assessments, providing a systematic approach to gathering data on a wide range of social, economic, and environmental factors. By using different types of surveys (cross-sectional, longitudinal) and designing both structured and semi-structured questionnaires, impact assessors can collect the necessary data to evaluate the potential impacts of a project. These tools ensure that the voices of diverse stakeholders are heard, and they contribute to making evidence-based decisions that minimize negative impacts and maximize positive outcomes for communities, ecosystems, and economies.

5.1.2 Interviews and Focus Groups in Impact Assessment

Interviews and focus groups are crucial methods in qualitative data collection for impact assessments. They offer an in-depth understanding of the experiences, perceptions, and attitudes of stakeholders, providing insights that quantitative methods, such as surveys and questionnaires, cannot capture fully. These techniques are particularly valuable when exploring the social, cultural, and psychological impacts of a project, as they allow for the collection of detailed personal and group-level information.

Interviews in Impact Assessment

Interviews are one-on-one interactions between an interviewer and a respondent, designed to elicit information on specific topics. The information gathered through interviews is typically rich, detailed, and nuanced, as they allow for a deeper exploration of the respondent's thoughts, experiences, and beliefs. Depending on the level of structure in the interview process, interviews can be categorized into structured, semi-structured, and unstructured formats.

1. Structured Interviews

A structured interview involves a set of predetermined questions that the interviewer asks in the same order and manner. Structured interviews are highly organized, and each interview is expected to be consistent, ensuring uniformity in data collection. This format is useful when the researcher wants to gather specific information and ensure comparability across different participants.

Characteristics:

• Predefined set of questions with fixed response options (e.g., yes/no, multiple choice).

• Questions are asked in the same order to all respondents.

• Little flexibility or room for deviation, focusing on consistency.

• Easy to analyze quantitatively due to the standardized nature of the responses.

Advantages:

Provides highly reliable and comparable data.

Efficient for collecting data on clearly defined topics.

Helps reduce interviewer bias because the questions and the response options are predefined.

Suitable for large-scale data collection if the survey is designed for a broad group of people.

Applications in Impact Assessment: Structured interviews are frequently used in the initial phases of an impact assessment to collect baseline data or to assess the specific effects of a project on target populations. For example, in an environmental impact assessment, a structured interview may be used to gather information about local residents' awareness of environmental issues such as pollution, waste disposal, and conservation efforts.

2. Semi-Structured Interviews

Semi-structured interviews are more flexible than structured ones. While there is still a set of guiding questions, the interviewer has the flexibility to explore certain topics in more depth based on the responses of the interviewee. This flexibility allows the interviewer to follow up on interesting or unexpected insights, which can lead to richer data collection.

Characteristics:

A mixture of predefined questions and the freedom to ask additional, unplanned questions based on the conversation.

Some flexibility in the order of the questions.

The interviewer can probe deeper into topics, providing a more comprehensive understanding of the interviewee's views.

Advantages:

Provides flexibility for exploration of unexpected topics or issues that emerge during the conversation.

Encourages a more conversational tone, which can help the respondent feel more comfortable sharing their views.

Allows the interviewer to clarify questions if the respondent does not understand them.

Useful for gathering detailed, qualitative insights into complex issues.

Applications in Impact Assessment: Semi-structured interviews are particularly useful in social impact assessments, where understanding the perceptions and experiences of the affected community is crucial. For example, during the assessment of a resettlement project, semi-structured interviews could be used to gather the personal experiences of individuals who are being relocated, exploring issues such as emotional stress, compensation adequacy, and community support.

3. Unstructured Interviews

Unstructured interviews are the most informal and open-ended type of interview. There is no predetermined set of questions; instead, the interviewer engages in a free-flowing conversation with the respondent. This format allows for a deep exploration of the respondent's perspectives and is particularly useful when the researcher wants to understand complex, multi-dimensional issues.

Characteristics:

No set questions: the conversation is guided by the respondent's responses.

Highly flexible and open-ended, with the potential to explore a wide range of topics.

Useful for gathering a broad range of information on issues that might not have been anticipated.

Advantages:

Provides the richest, most in-depth data.

Enables the interviewer to explore topics that emerge organically during the conversation.

Useful for understanding the broader context and personal feelings of respondents, especially when dealing with sensitive topics.

Applications in Impact Assessment: Unstructured interviews are particularly useful in assessing the psychological and emotional impacts of projects. For example, in a development project that displaces people, unstructured interviews can help capture the emotional and social costs of displacement, including community identity, loss of livelihoods, and mental health challenges, which may not be fully captured by more structured methods.

Focus Groups in Impact Assessment

Focus groups are another qualitative method used in impact assessments. A focus group is a facilitated discussion with a small group of participants, typically 6 to 12 people, who share their views on a specific topic or issue. The group discussion is guided by a facilitator, who ensures that all participants have the opportunity to contribute. Focus groups are useful for exploring how a particular group of people feels about an issue, generating ideas, or validating the findings of other data collection methods.

Characteristics of Focus Groups

Group Interaction: The discussion occurs in a group setting, which can stimulate new ideas and allow participants to react to each other's opinions. This interaction can lead to deeper insights than individual interviews.

Moderated Discussion: A trained facilitator guides the discussion, ensuring that the conversation stays on topic and that all participants have the opportunity to share their views.

Homogeneity of Participants: Participants are often selected based on common characteristics or shared experiences (e.g., residents of the same area, employees of the same company). This helps ensure that the discussion is relevant to all group members.

Advantages of Focus Groups

Rich Data: Focus groups can generate more detailed and nuanced data because participants can build on each other's ideas, leading to a deeper exploration of topics.

Exploratory: Focus groups are ideal for exploring new topics, testing hypotheses, and understanding the collective views of a group.

Stimulates New Ideas: The group dynamic can encourage participants to consider perspectives they may not have thought of individually, leading to new insights and solutions.

Efficient Use of Time: Focus groups allow for the collection of multiple perspectives at once, making them more time-efficient than individual interviews.

Applications in Impact Assessment

Focus groups are widely used in social impact assessments to explore community perceptions, concerns, and attitudes toward a project. They can help assess the social dynamics of a community and identify potential sources of conflict or resistance to the project. For instance, in a road construction project, a focus group of local residents could provide insights into their views on traffic safety, changes in access to services, or the potential benefits of improved infrastructure.

Application of Interviews and Focus Groups in Impact Assessment

Both interviews and focus groups can be particularly useful in the following contexts of impact assessments:

Exploring Community Perceptions: These techniques provide a platform for community members to express their views on the project and discuss their concerns. By allowing participants to speak in their own words, interviews and focus groups offer deeper insights into the community's attitudes toward the project.

Understanding Social and Cultural Dynamics: Interviews and focus groups are useful when the project might have complex social or cultural impacts. They can help assess how the project will affect cultural practices, social networks, or local traditions. For example, in a project that affects indigenous communities, these methods can be used to explore the cultural significance of land or resources and understand the potential consequences of displacement.

Validating and Complementing Other Data: Interviews and focus groups can be used to validate or complement the findings from quantitative surveys or environmental assessments. For example, if a survey identifies potential environmental impacts, focus groups can be used to explore the community's concerns and perceptions about these impacts in more detail.

Testing Hypotheses: These methods can help researchers test hypotheses that arise from other parts of the impact assessment. For example, if a survey indicates that the project may have economic benefits, focus groups can help test whether local businesses perceive these benefits in the same way.

Challenges and Considerations

While interviews and focus groups provide rich qualitative data, there are several challenges and considerations to be aware of:

Sampling Bias: Careful attention must be given to selecting participants who represent the diversity of views within the community. Bias in sampling can skew the results.

Interviewer Bias: The interviewer's opinions or behaviors can influence the responses of participants. Training interviewers and focus group facilitators is essential to minimize this bias.

Data Analysis: Analyzing qualitative data from interviews and focus groups can be time-consuming and complex. It requires coding and identifying themes, patterns, and connections between responses.

Privacy and Confidentiality: In sensitive areas such as resettlement or displacement, it is essential to ensure that participants feel safe and comfortable sharing their views. Confidentiality should be maintained to protect the privacy of participants.

Interviews and focus groups are invaluable tools in impact assessments, offering a deep and nuanced understanding of the social, cultural, and psychological factors that influence project outcomes. By using structured, semi-structured, or unstructured interviews, or organizing focus groups, researchers can capture rich, qualitative data that informs the assessment of social, environmental, and economic impacts. When combined with other methods such as surveys or Participatory Rural Appraisal, interviews and focus groups contribute to a holistic understanding of the impacts of a project and help ensure that decision-making is grounded in the perspectives and experiences of affected communities.

5.2.1 Geographic Information Systems (GIS)

Geographic Information Systems (GIS) are powerful tools that combine spatial data and advanced analytical capabilities to understand the patterns and dynamics within geographic areas. These systems are essential in the modern practice of environmental and socio-economic impact assessments, providing spatial data that allows researchers, planners, and decision-makers to visualize and interpret geographic phenomena in a structured, data-driven manner.

Overview of GIS

GIS refers to a set of computer-based tools used to capture, store, analyze, manage, and visualize spatial and geographic data. It enables users to create layered maps that integrate different data types, such as satellite images, aerial photographs, survey data, field observations, and historical data. These maps provide insights into various aspects of the environment, socio-economic conditions, and infrastructure. GIS is particularly effective in analyzing spatial patterns and geographic factors that influence the outcomes of a project or development initiative.

A GIS typically works by representing geographic features through maps, tables, charts, and databases. These representations are linked to specific geographic locations using coordinates (latitude and longitude). GIS also includes tools for spatial analysis, which can be used to model and predict the outcomes of different scenarios, based on the analysis of spatial data.

Applications of GIS in Impact Assessment

1. Environmental Mapping

GIS is widely used in environmental assessments to map and visualize sensitive environmental areas that may be impacted by a project. Environmental mapping in GIS can provide detailed, spatially accurate information on key ecological features, including forests, wetlands, wildlife habitats, and water bodies. This information is essential for assessing the potential impacts of a project on biodiversity, ecosystems, and natural resources. By integrating remote sensing data and field observations, GIS can map out the extent of forests, wetlands, or protected areas and identify any potential environmental risks posed by the project.

For example, in the construction of a new road, GIS can map out the proximity of the planned route to protected forest areas or water bodies. This spatial information helps in identifying risks of habitat destruction, soil erosion, or water contamination from the road's construction activities.

Additionally, GIS tools can help prioritize mitigation measures, such as rerouting or creating buffer zones around sensitive areas, ensuring that the project minimizes its ecological footprint.

2. Land Use and Zoning Analysis

One of the primary applications of GIS in impact assessment is the analysis of land use patterns and zoning regulations. GIS tools can map existing land use in the project area, including agricultural, residential, commercial, industrial, and recreational spaces. This mapping allows planners to understand how the proposed project fits within the broader landscape and its impact on surrounding communities and ecosystems.

Land use data can be overlaid with zoning regulations to identify areas where land use changes are permissible and areas that are subject to restrictions due to environmental or regulatory concerns. For instance, GIS can be used to visualize how a proposed industrial facility would impact nearby residential or agricultural areas. Understanding the spatial relationship between different land uses is essential for planning infrastructure, transportation networks, and community services that minimize conflict and promote sustainable development.

Furthermore, GIS can track changes in land use over time. This is valuable for assessing trends in urbanization, deforestation, agricultural expansion, and other factors that may influence the environmental and social outcomes of the project. For instance, if a road construction project is planned in an area that has been steadily converting from agricultural to urban land, GIS can identify potential impacts on local food production, wildlife, and the availability of natural resources.

3. Vulnerability and Risk Assessment

Another critical application of GIS in impact assessment is vulnerability and risk analysis. GIS can be used to identify and map areas that are vulnerable to environmental or social impacts caused by a project. This includes assessing the risk of flooding, landslides, erosion, or other natural hazards.

For example, GIS can be used to analyze the potential for flooding in a coastal area by overlaying elevation data with weather patterns and flood-prone zones. It can also assess the vulnerability of populations living in areas at risk of environmental hazards, such as toxic spills or earthquakes. By identifying these vulnerable areas, planners and decision-makers can implement targeted mitigation strategies to reduce the impact on communities and the environment.

Moreover, GIS tools can combine multiple layers of data to assess the cumulative impacts of a project. For instance, GIS can evaluate how different environmental factors, such as soil type, vegetation, and rainfall, interact to increase or decrease the risk of landslides or erosion. This allows for a more comprehensive and accurate understanding of project risks and helps in developing appropriate mitigation measures.

4. Community Impact and Social Analysis

GIS is also valuable in understanding the social dynamics and community impacts of a project. It allows for the spatial analysis of demographic data, such as population density, income levels, education, health, and other socio-economic indicators. By analyzing these factors spatially, GIS helps identify communities that may be disproportionately impacted by a project. For example, if a new transportation project is planned in a densely populated urban area, GIS can be used to assess how the project will affect access to schools, healthcare, and employment opportunities. It can also identify vulnerable populations, such as low-income households or marginalized communities, and evaluate the potential social benefits or harms of the project.

In addition, GIS can help track the distribution of social services and infrastructure, ensuring that new developments or improvements are equitable and accessible to all members of the community. This spatial analysis of social factors is essential for designing projects that promote inclusivity and reduce disparities.

5.2.2 Remote Sensing

Remote sensing refers to the process of collecting data about the Earth's surface from a distance, typically using satellites, drones, or aircraft. This technology provides invaluable insights into the landscape and environment, making it an essential tool for impact assessments. Remote sensing data is often integrated with GIS for more comprehensive spatial analysis and visualization.

Remote sensing provides a broader, more dynamic view of the land, enabling the monitoring of changes in land cover, vegetation, water bodies, and other environmental factors over time. Unlike ground-based methods, remote sensing can cover large areas and collect data in real-time, which is essential for monitoring changes during project implementation.

Applications of Remote Sensing in Impact Assessment

1. Monitoring Land Use Changes

Remote sensing is highly effective in tracking changes in land cover and land use over time. This can be critical in understanding the environmental impacts of a project, particularly in terms of deforestation, urban expansion, or agricultural conversion. Remote sensing provides continuous, high-resolution imagery that can be used to detect subtle changes in land cover, such as the conversion of forested areas to agricultural land or the expansion of urban sprawl.

For example, in an environmental impact assessment of a new industrial development, remote sensing data can be used to track how land use has evolved in the project area over the past few decades. By comparing historical satellite images, planners can assess trends and anticipate potential long-term impacts of the project on the landscape and surrounding ecosystems.

Furthermore, remote sensing can be used to detect illegal land use activities, such as illegal logging or encroachment into protected areas, which may not be easily visible through ground surveys alone. This makes remote sensing a valuable tool for enforcing environmental regulations and monitoring compliance.

2. Vegetation and Biodiversity Monitoring

Remote sensing is particularly useful for monitoring vegetation and biodiversity in the project area. Satellite imagery and aerial photographs can provide detailed information on vegetation cover, forest density, and species diversity. This data can be used to assess the health of ecosystems and identify areas of high biodiversity that may need to be protected from development.

In biodiversity monitoring, remote sensing can help detect changes in vegetation density and forest cover, which are indicators of ecosystem degradation. For example, a rapid decline in vegetation cover due to deforestation or land conversion can be detected early using remote sensing techniques. This allows stakeholders to implement conservation measures before significant damage is done.

Additionally, remote sensing data can help identify areas with high biodiversity value, such as critical wildlife corridors or endangered species habitats. This information is essential for ensuring that development projects do not disrupt these sensitive ecosystems.

3. Environmental Degradation Monitoring

Remote sensing is also a valuable tool for detecting and monitoring signs of environmental degradation, such as deforestation, soil erosion, and pollution. Satellite imagery can capture large-scale environmental changes, including the spread of pollutants, water contamination, or soil erosion in mining or construction areas.

For example, remote sensing can be used to monitor the impact of agricultural practices on soil health. By analyzing satellite images over time, it is possible to detect changes in vegetation cover and soil moisture levels, which may indicate soil erosion or degradation. Similarly, remote sensing can track the spread of pollution, such as oil spills or chemical runoff, by identifying changes in water bodies' color and turbidity.

4. Climate Change Monitoring

Remote sensing is essential for tracking climate change impacts, particularly in terms of changes in land cover, temperature, and precipitation patterns. Satellite data can monitor shifting weather patterns, such as increased rainfall or rising temperatures, and their effects on ecosystems, agriculture, and water resources.

For example, remote sensing can be used to assess the impact of changing rainfall patterns on crop yields in agricultural regions. It can also monitor glacial retreat, sea-level rise, and other signs of climate change, providing valuable information for decision-making in project planning and mitigation.

GIS and remote sensing are indispensable tools in environmental and socio-economic impact assessments. GIS provides spatial analysis and visualization capabilities, enabling the identification of environmental, social, and economic patterns in the project area. Remote sensing, on the other hand, offers a broad view of the landscape and allows for monitoring changes over time, providing real-time data on environmental degradation, land use, and biodiversity.

By integrating both GIS and remote sensing data, practitioners can develop a comprehensive understanding of a project's potential impacts, design effective mitigation measures, and ensure that the development is sustainable and beneficial to both the environment and the communities it affects. As the demand for more efficient and data-driven decision-making increases, the role of GIS and remote sensing in impact assessment will continue to grow, offering powerful tools for assessing, monitoring, and managing the environmental and social consequences of development projects.

5.3 Statistical Analysis and Modeling Tools in Impact Assessment

Statistical analysis and modelling tools play a pivotal role in impact assessments by enabling the quantification of potential impacts, predicting future outcomes under various scenarios, and helping stakeholders make informed decisions. These tools, when applied correctly, can provide valuable insights into the social, economic, and environmental effects of projects, helping policymakers, planners, and practitioners design more sustainable and effective interventions.

The combination of statistical analysis and modelling enables practitioners to not only understand the data collected during an impact assessment but also forecast the potential consequences of different project scenarios. This ability is essential for mitigating risks, optimizing resource allocation, and enhancing the overall effectiveness of a project.

5.3.1 Statistical Analysis in Impact Assessment

Statistical analysis involves applying mathematical techniques to summarize, interpret, and draw conclusions from collected data. In impact assessments, statistical analysis is used to quantify impacts, identify trends, and evaluate the relationships between different factors. It allows for the translation of raw data into meaningful information that can inform decision-making processes.

Types of Statistical Techniques Used in Impact Assessment

1. Descriptive Statistics

Descriptive statistics are foundational techniques used to summarize and describe the main features of a data set. These techniques help in providing an overview of the data, allowing researchers to easily interpret and understand the key characteristics of the sample population or geographic area being studied.

Common descriptive statistics include:

Mean: The average value of a set of data points, used to determine the central tendency of the data.

Median: The middle value in a data set when it is ordered, providing an alternative to the mean, particularly useful when data sets include outliers.

Mode: The most frequent value in the data set, often used to identify trends or popular categories.

Standard Deviation: A measure of how spread out the values in a data set are around the mean. It helps in understanding the variability or consistency of the data.

Frequency Distributions: A summary of the occurrence of different values or ranges of values in the data. Frequency distributions are commonly displayed in histograms, bar charts, or tables.

These descriptive statistics are essential for summarizing large datasets and identifying trends or outliers that may require further analysis.

2. Inferential Statistics

Inferential statistics are techniques that allow researchers to make predictions or generalizations about a population based on a sample. These methods are crucial in impact assessments because they help in drawing conclusions about the broader population or project area based on a limited amount of data.

Key inferential statistical techniques include:

Hypothesis Testing: This technique is used to test the validity of a hypothesis or assumption. For example, in an impact assessment, a hypothesis could be that a new road will reduce travel time for local residents. Hypothesis testing evaluates whether the data support this assumption or whether the observed effect could have occurred by chance.

Confidence Intervals: A confidence interval provides a range of values within which the true population parameter is likely to fall. For instance, when predicting the economic benefits of a project, a confidence interval can help in expressing the uncertainty around the estimated outcomes.

Regression Analysis: Regression analysis helps determine the relationship between dependent and independent variables. It is used in impact assessments to analyze how changes in one factor, such as an increase in pollution levels, affect another, such as the health outcomes of a population. Linear regression and multiple regression are commonly used techniques in this area.

Inferential statistics allow researchers to extend the findings from a sample to a larger population and make predictions about future impacts.

3. Multivariate Analysis

Multivariate analysis techniques are used when there are multiple variables that may interact with one another and influence the outcomes of a project. These techniques help in identifying patterns, relationships, and interactions among different factors, and are especially useful in complex impact assessments where several variables affect each other simultaneously.

Key multivariate techniques used in impact assessments include:

Factor Analysis: This technique reduces the number of variables by grouping them into underlying factors. For example, if a study collects data on various environmental variables (air quality, water quality, biodiversity, etc.), factor analysis can help identify the major environmental factors that influence project outcomes.

Cluster Analysis: Cluster analysis is used to group similar data points into clusters based on their characteristics. In impact assessments, cluster analysis can be used to identify communities with similar socio-economic characteristics or environmental conditions, allowing for tailored interventions or policies.

Principal Component Analysis (PCA): PCA is a technique used to reduce the dimensionality of data by transforming the original variables into a smaller set of uncorrelated variables (principal components). PCA is particularly useful when analyzing large datasets with many variables, helping to identify the most important drivers of change.

Multivariate analysis techniques allow practitioners to handle complex data and gain insights into how different factors work together to influence project outcomes.

5.3.2 Modeling Tools in Impact Assessment

Modeling tools are essential in simulating complex systems and predicting the potential outcomes of various scenarios. In impact assessments, models help forecast the effects of a project under different assumptions and conditions, providing decision-makers with the necessary information to evaluate the long-term consequences of their actions.

Models are used to simulate environmental, economic, and social processes, allowing for the prediction of impacts over time and under different conditions. By using modeling tools, practitioners can test various hypotheses and understand how different variables interact in a system.

Types of Models Used in Impact Assessment

1. Environmental Models

Environmental models are used to simulate environmental processes and predict the potential impacts of a project on the environment. These models can help forecast the effects of pollution, habitat destruction, climate change, and other environmental factors.

Key types of environmental models include:

Air Quality Models: These models simulate the dispersion of pollutants in the atmosphere. They can predict the concentrations of pollutants (such as particulate matter, nitrogen oxides, and sulfur dioxide) in the air over time and under different conditions. For example, an air quality model can be used to assess the impact of a new industrial facility on local air quality and public health.

Hydrological Models: Hydrological models simulate the movement and distribution of water in the environment, helping to predict the impact of a project on water resources. These models can be used to assess changes in river flow, groundwater levels, or water quality due to construction activities, land use changes, or climate change. They are crucial in flood risk assessment and water resource management.

Climate Models: Climate models simulate the interactions between various factors that influence the Earth's climate, such as greenhouse gas emissions, temperature, and precipitation patterns. These models help in predicting the long-term impacts of climate change on ecosystems and human communities. In impact assessments, climate models are used to forecast how a project may contribute to or mitigate climate change.

Environmental models provide valuable information for understanding how a project will impact natural resources, ecosystems, and climate patterns.

2. Economic Models

Economic models are used to assess the economic impacts of a project, including changes in employment, income, and the local economy. These models simulate the effects of various economic variables on the community and region and help predict how the project will affect economic indicators such as GDP, wages, and business activity.

Common economic models used in impact assessments include:

Input-Output Models: These models simulate the flow of goods and services in an economy by mapping the interconnections between different industries and sectors. Input-output models are useful for assessing how a project (such as the construction of infrastructure) will affect various industries, including construction, transportation, manufacturing, and services.

Econometric Models: Econometric models use statistical methods to model the relationships between different economic variables, such as employment, income, and consumption. These models help in predicting the economic effects of a project by estimating how changes in one variable will affect others. For example, an econometric model can be used to assess how the construction of a new road will influence employment rates and business revenues in surrounding areas.

Cost-Benefit Analysis (CBA): Cost-benefit analysis is a key economic modeling technique used to assess the overall value of a project. By comparing the projected costs (e.g., construction costs, environmental mitigation) with the anticipated benefits (e.g., increased productivity, job creation), CBA helps to determine whether a project will deliver net positive economic returns.

Economic models help stakeholders understand the financial and economic viability of a project and predict its potential long-term effects on local economies.

3. Social Models

Social models are used to simulate the social impacts of a project on communities, including effects on health, education, social well-being, and cultural factors. These models help assess how a project will influence social indicators and forecast potential changes in community dynamics.

Social models are often used in social impact assessments (SIAs) and can include:

Health Impact Assessment Models: These models simulate the effects of a project on public health outcomes, such as changes in disease prevalence, health care access, or mortality rates. For example, a health impact model can be used to predict the effects of air pollution from a new industrial facility on respiratory diseases in nearby communities.

Education Models: Education models predict the impact of a project on access to education and learning outcomes. These models are useful in assessing how changes in infrastructure, such as building new schools or improving transportation networks, will affect school enrollment rates and educational attainment.

Social Well-being Models: These models assess how a project affects the overall well-being of a community, including factors such as quality of life, social cohesion, and cultural preservation. They are particularly useful in understanding the broader social impacts of large development projects on local populations.

Social models help to predict changes in health, education, and social cohesion, providing valuable insights into the social consequences of a project.

Statistical analysis and modeling tools are integral components of impact assessments, helping to quantify potential impacts, identify trends, and forecast future outcomes. Statistical techniques, such as descriptive statistics, inferential statistics, and multivariate analysis, allow for the effective interpretation of data and the drawing of meaningful conclusions. Modeling tools, including environmental, economic, and social models, help simulate complex systems and predict the long-term effects of a project on different aspects of society, the economy, and the environment.

The combination of statistical analysis and modeling provides decision-makers with a robust framework for evaluating the potential consequences of development projects, enabling more informed, evidence-based decisions. By using these tools, practitioners can ensure that projects are designed and implemented in a way that maximizes benefits while minimizing negative impacts, contributing to more sustainable development outcomes.

5.5 Impact Scoring and Ranking Techniques

Impact scoring and ranking techniques are used to assess and prioritize the significance of various project impacts. These techniques involve assigning numerical values or scores to different impacts based on their severity, likelihood, and importance.

5.5.1 Scoring Techniques

Impact scoring involves assigning scores to different project impacts based on predefined criteria, such as their magnitude, duration, and reversibility. The scores are typically numerical, and impacts are ranked accordingly.

5.5.2 Ranking Techniques

Ranking techniques are used to prioritize impacts based on their significance. Impacts are ranked from most to least significant, helping decision-makers focus on the most critical issues.

5.5 Impact Scoring and Ranking Techniques in Impact Assessment

Impact scoring and ranking are essential techniques used in the assessment process to evaluate and prioritize the significance of various project impacts. They provide a systematic method to assess potential impacts based on various criteria such as their severity, likelihood, and importance. By assigning numerical scores and rankings to different impacts, these techniques help decision-makers understand which impacts require the most attention, guiding them to design mitigation strategies and resource allocation effectively. These methodologies are particularly useful in managing the complexity of large-scale development projects where multiple potential impacts—environmental, social, and economic—are involved.

This section discusses the principles and applications of impact scoring and ranking techniques, providing a detailed explanation of their roles, types, and implementation in the context of impact assessment.

5.5.1 Scoring Techniques in Impact Assessment

Impact scoring involves assigning numerical values to different impacts based on predefined criteria. This quantitative approach helps in evaluating the severity, likelihood, and importance of impacts in a way that facilitates comparison and prioritization. Scoring techniques are used to quantify the impacts of a project across multiple dimensions, such as environmental, social, economic, and cultural aspects.

Key Elements of Scoring Techniques

Scoring techniques are based on a set of criteria that reflect the significance of an impact. These criteria typically include the following:

Magnitude (Severity) of Impact: The magnitude or severity of an impact refers to how large or intense the effect of the project will be. For example, in an environmental assessment, the magnitude of an impact could relate to the extent of habitat destruction, air pollution, or water contamination. Impacts with higher magnitudes usually receive higher scores, indicating their greater significance.

Duration of Impact: This criterion refers to how long the impact is expected to last. Impacts can be short-term (temporary), medium-term, or long-term (permanent). Permanent impacts typically receive higher scores than temporary ones due to their lasting consequences.

Reversibility of Impact: This refers to whether an impact can be reversed or mitigated once it occurs. Irreversible or difficult-to-reverse impacts, such as species extinction or land degradation, are given higher scores due to their long-lasting effects.

Likelihood of Occurrence: This criterion estimates the probability that the impact will occur. Impacts with a high likelihood of occurrence are assigned higher scores, reflecting the increased need for mitigation measures.

Importance of Impact: This criterion involves assessing the significance of an impact from a stakeholder perspective. For example, social impacts like displacement or loss of livelihood may be considered more significant by local communities, even if their magnitude is smaller compared to environmental impacts.

Common Scoring Systems

Various scoring systems can be used to quantify impacts based on the above criteria. A few common methods include:

Simple Numerical Scoring: Impacts are assigned scores from a fixed range (for example, 1 to 5, where 1 represents a low impact and 5 represents a high impact). Each impact is evaluated across different criteria (magnitude, duration, etc.), and an overall score is calculated by adding or averaging the individual scores.

Weighted Scoring System: In this system, each criterion is assigned a weight that reflects its relative importance. For example, environmental impacts may be considered more critical than economic impacts in some projects. After assigning scores to individual impacts, these scores are multiplied by the weights to obtain a weighted score, which helps prioritize the most significant impacts.

Risk Matrix Scoring: A risk matrix is used to score impacts based on their likelihood and severity. For example, impacts that have a high likelihood of occurrence and high severity may be scored as "high-risk" and require immediate attention. A color-coded matrix (e.g., green for low risk, yellow for medium risk, red for high risk) is often used for visual clarity.

Application of Scoring Techniques

Scoring techniques are widely used in environmental and social impact assessments, particularly in large-scale infrastructure projects. For example, in the context of road construction, scoring techniques can be used to assess the potential impacts on air quality, local wildlife, traffic congestion, social cohesion, and public health. By assigning scores to these different impacts, decision-makers can identify which areas require mitigation measures and allocate resources accordingly.

For example, consider the case of a road construction project in a rural area. The potential impacts may include habitat destruction (high severity, long-term, irreversible), air pollution (moderate severity, short-term, reversible), and improved access to healthcare (low severity, long-term, positive). Each of these impacts would be scored on various criteria, and their overall scores would help prioritize the most pressing issues that need to be addressed during the project's planning and implementation phases.

5.5.3 Benefits and Challenges of Scoring and Ranking Techniques

Benefits

Improved Decision-Making: Scoring and ranking techniques provide a systematic and transparent approach to evaluating and prioritizing project impacts. This helps decision-makers focus on the most critical issues and make informed choices about mitigation and management strategies.

Resource Optimization: By prioritizing the most significant impacts, scoring and ranking help ensure that resources (time, money, and effort) are allocated to areas where they will have the greatest effect.

Stakeholder Engagement: These techniques often involve input from stakeholders, which helps ensure that the impacts that matter most to local communities, environmental groups, and other relevant parties are given adequate attention.

Clear Communication: Scoring and ranking impacts allow for clear communication of the relative significance of different impacts, facilitating discussions among stakeholders and improving transparency in decision-making.

Subjectivity: Scoring and ranking techniques can sometimes be subjective, especially when different stakeholders have differing opinions on the severity or importance of an impact. To mitigate this, the process should involve diverse stakeholder input and be based on clear, objective criteria.

Data Limitations: Accurate scoring and ranking depend on high-quality data. Incomplete or uncertain data can affect the reliability of the scores and rankings, potentially leading to misinformed decisions.

Complexity in Large Projects: In large-scale projects with numerous potential impacts, scoring and ranking can become complex. Managing and analyzing large amounts of data requires careful planning and sophisticated tools to ensure that the process remains manageable.

Impact scoring and ranking techniques are essential tools in the impact assessment process, providing a structured approach to evaluating and prioritizing the potential impacts of a project. By assigning scores based on predefined criteria and ranking impacts according to their significance, these techniques help ensure that decision-makers address the most critical issues first. While scoring and ranking techniques have many benefits, including improved decision-making, resource optimization, and stakeholder engagement, they also face challenges related to subjectivity, data limitations, and complexity. When applied effectively, these techniques contribute significantly to the sustainability and success of development projects by guiding the implementation of appropriate mitigation measures and promoting better outcomes for all stakeholders involved.

Conclusion

In conclusion, the tools and techniques outlined in this chapter—ranging from data collection and GIS to statistical analysis, modelling, and impact scoring—are essential for conducting comprehensive and accurate impact assessments. By combining these methods, practitioners can create a well-rounded analysis of potential project impacts, ensuring that decision-making is informed by reliable, evidence-based data. These tools not only support the identification of key issues and potential risks but also facilitate the development of effective mitigation strategies that enhance the overall sustainability of projects.

Moreover, these techniques foster greater stakeholder engagement and transparency, ensuring that all relevant parties are informed and involved in the decision-making process. Ultimately, the goal is to design projects that are both beneficial and sustainable, minimizing negative impacts while maximizing social, environmental, and economic gains for all stakeholders involved.

CHAPTER VI

Data Gaps and Limitations in Impact Assessment

Impact assessments vary significantly depending on the nature of the sector in which a project is being implemented. Each sector has unique characteristics, challenges, and stakeholders, requiring tailored approaches to evaluating potential impacts. This chapter explores sector-specific impact assessments across six critical domains: infrastructure and transportation, energy and power, industrial and manufacturing, agriculture and rural development, urban development and smart cities, and water, sanitation, and waste management projects.

These assessments ensure that the projects not only achieve their objectives but also align with principles of environmental sustainability, social equity, and economic inclusivity.

6.1 Infrastructure and Transportation Projects

Infrastructure and transportation projects play a pivotal role in fostering economic growth, enhancing connectivity, and improving access to essential services. From highways and railways to ports and airports, these projects form the arteries of national and global economies. Despite their numerous benefits, the far-reaching environmental, social, and economic impacts of infrastructure and transportation projects necessitate a comprehensive and nuanced approach to impact assessment. This section delves deeper into the key impacts, tools, and mitigation strategies associated with such projects.

6.1.1 Key Impacts of Infrastructure and Transportation Projects

Environmental Impacts

Infrastructure and transportation projects can significantly alter the natural landscape and ecosystem. Key environmental challenges include:

Habitat Destruction and Biodiversity Loss:

Land acquisition for roads, railways, or airports often results in deforestation and fragmentation of habitats. This disrupts local wildlife populations, endangering species and reducing biodiversity.

Sensitive ecosystems, such as wetlands and mangroves, are particularly vulnerable.

Soil Erosion and Land Degradation:

Construction activities disturb the soil structure, making it prone to erosion.

Quarrying for construction materials further depletes land resources.

Air and Noise Pollution:

Increased vehicular traffic leads to higher emissions of greenhouse gases (GHGs) and particulate matter, contributing to climate change and poor air quality.

Construction equipment and vehicles generate noise pollution, affecting local communities and wildlife.

Water Resource Contamination:

Runoff from construction sites can carry pollutants into water bodies, harming aquatic ecosystems.

Social Impacts

While infrastructure projects can bring immense social benefits, they also pose risks to communities:

Displacement and Resettlement:

Large-scale land acquisition often results in the displacement of communities, disrupting their lives and livelihoods.

Vulnerable populations, such as indigenous groups, bear a disproportionate burden.

Inequality and Social Cohesion:

Projects designed without inclusivity can exacerbate social inequality, favoring urban or affluent populations over rural or marginalized groups.

Health and Safety Concerns:

Construction activities and vehicular emissions can lead to respiratory issues and other health problems among nearby populations.

Accidents during construction or operation phases pose risks to workers and the public.

Economic Impacts

Infrastructure projects stimulate local and national economies, but their economic viability and sustainability must be carefully evaluated:

Job Creation and Economic Growth:

Infrastructure development generates employment during construction and operation phases, boosting local economies.

Improved connectivity facilitates trade and commerce.

Impact on Local Businesses:

Projects can create opportunities for small businesses but may also displace existing enterprises or disrupt local supply chains.

Long-Term Economic Viability:

The benefits of infrastructure projects depend on their integration into broader development plans. Poorly designed projects can become financial burdens.

6.1.2 Assessment Tools and Approaches

1. Geographic Information Systems (GIS) and Remote Sensing

Route Optimization: GIS tools help in designing routes that minimize environmental and social disruptions by avoiding sensitive areas like forests or wetlands.

Impact Visualization: Remote sensing provides a bird's-eye view of the project area, enabling stakeholders to visualize potential impacts.

2. Traffic and Economic Models

Demand Forecasting: Traffic models predict the flow of vehicles, helping planners assess the necessity and scale of the project.

Economic Analysis: Models such as cost-benefit analysis (CBA) estimate the economic returns of the project and its impact on local and national economies.

3. Social Impact Assessments (SIA)

Community Consultations: Engaging with affected communities ensures their concerns are addressed and benefits are equitably distributed.

Livelihood Restoration Plans: Assessments focus on providing alternative livelihoods for displaced populations.

4. Environmental Impact Assessments (EIA)

Biodiversity Surveys: EIAs identify sensitive species and ecosystems that require protection.

Mitigation Strategies: EIAs propose measures to reduce environmental harm.

6.1.3 Mitigation Measures

To balance development with sustainability, infrastructure and transportation projects should incorporate the following mitigation measures:

1. Green Infrastructure Solutions

Eco-Bridges and Wildlife Corridors: These structures allow wildlife to safely cross roads or railways, minimizing habitat fragmentation.

Permeable Surfaces: Using permeable materials in construction reduces runoff and enhances groundwater recharge.

2. Resettlement and Rehabilitation Plans

Fair Compensation: Displaced communities should receive adequate financial compensation and access to alternative housing and livelihoods.

Community Participation: Involving affected populations in planning and decision-making fosters trust and ensures equitable outcomes.

3. Sustainable Transportation Integration

Public Transportation: Developing bus rapid transit (BRT) systems, metro lines, or cycling tracks minimizes reliance on personal vehicles, reducing emissions.

Electric and Low-Emission Vehicles: Encouraging the use of electric or hybrid vehicles reduces the carbon footprint of transportation networks.

4. Policy and Regulatory Frameworks

Environmental Regulations: Enforcing stringent standards for emissions, noise, and waste management ensures compliance with sustainability goals.

Land Use Planning: Coordinating infrastructure development with urban and rural planning minimizes conflicts and maximizes efficiency.

6.1.4 Case Studies

1. Golden Quadrilateral Project, India

The highway network connecting major cities has boosted trade and reduced travel time.

However, the project faced challenges like deforestation and displacement, highlighting the need for robust mitigation strategies.

2. Cross-rail Project, London, UK

The urban rail network improved connectivity and economic activity.

Extensive community engagement and adherence to environmental standards ensured minimal negative impacts.

3. Bogota's Trans-Milenio BRT System

This bus rapid transit system reduced traffic congestion and vehicular emissions in Colombia's capital.

Investments in public transportation provided affordable mobility options for low-income groups.

6.1.5 Emerging Trends in Infrastructure and Transportation Impact Assessment

Smart Infrastructure: Incorporating IoT and AI for real-time monitoring and maintenance reduces costs and environmental impacts.

Sustainable Financing: Green bonds and other financial instruments are increasingly used to fund eco-friendly projects.

Climate Resilience: Designing infrastructure to withstand extreme weather events ensures long-term sustainability.

Infrastructure and transportation projects are critical for economic and social development, but they must be implemented responsibly to mitigate adverse impacts. By leveraging advanced tools like GIS and remote sensing, engaging stakeholders through social impact assessments, and adopting sustainable practices, these projects can achieve their objectives while safeguarding the environment and communities. A holistic approach that integrates environmental, social, and economic considerations ensures that infrastructure development contributes to a sustainable and equitable future.

6.2 Energy and Power Sector

The energy and power sector is at the forefront of modern development, supplying the energy required to fuel industries, power homes, and sustain technological advancements. It encompasses a wide range of projects, including renewable energy sources such as solar, wind, hydropower, and geothermal, as well as non-renewable sources like coal, oil, natural gas, and nuclear power. While these projects are critical to meeting the growing global energy demand and addressing climate change, they also present complex environmental, social, and economic challenges. This section explores the key impacts of energy projects, the tools used for their assessment, and the measures required to mitigate adverse effects while maximizing benefits.

6.2.1 Key Impacts of Energy and Power Projects

1. Environmental Impacts

Non-Renewable Energy Projects:

Air Pollution: Fossil fuel-based power plants release significant quantities of pollutants such as sulfur dioxide (SO_2), nitrogen oxides (NO_x), particulate matter, and greenhouse gases (GHGs), contributing to climate change and respiratory illnesses.

Water Contamination: Thermal power plants require large volumes of water for cooling, leading to thermal pollution and contamination of nearby water sources.

Land and Habitat Destruction: Mining for coal or drilling for oil often leads to deforestation, habitat loss, and soil degradation.

Renewable Energy Projects:

Land Use Changes: Solar farms require large areas, potentially leading to land use conflicts and habitat disruption.

Biodiversity Impacts: Wind turbines can affect bird and bat populations, while hydropower dams can disrupt aquatic ecosystems and fish migration patterns.

Resource Use: Manufacturing solar panels and wind turbines involves the extraction of rare earth metals, which can have localized environmental impacts.

2. Social Impacts

Displacement and Land Rights: Large-scale energy projects often require significant land acquisition, leading to the displacement of local populations and potential conflicts over land rights.

Livelihood Disruption: Communities dependent on natural resources for their livelihoods, such as agriculture or fishing, may face economic losses due to land acquisition or ecosystem changes.

Energy Access and Equity: While energy projects aim to improve access to electricity, inequities in distribution may leave marginalized groups underserved.

3. Economic Impacts

Job Creation: Both renewable and non-renewable energy projects generate employment during construction, operation, and maintenance phases.

Industrial Growth: Reliable energy supply is a key driver of industrial development, attracting investments and boosting economic growth.

Energy Tariffs: While renewable energy sources often reduce long-term costs, initial investments can lead to higher energy tariffs, affecting affordability for lower-income households.

6.2.2 Assessment Tools and Approaches

1. Life Cycle Assessment (LCA)

Purpose: LCA evaluates the environmental impacts of energy projects throughout their lifecycle, from resource extraction to decommissioning.

Application:

Assessing carbon footprints of different energy technologies.

Identifying areas for improvement in renewable energy production.

2. Environmental Impact Assessment (EIA)

Focus Areas:

Emissions and air quality monitoring for coal and gas plants.

Water resource management for hydropower and thermal plants.

Biodiversity studies for wind farms and solar installations.

Outputs:

Detailed impact reports outlining mitigation measures.

Public consultation processes to address community concerns.

3. Cost-Benefit Analysis (CBA)

Purpose: CBA evaluates the economic feasibility of energy projects by comparing costs (e.g., construction, maintenance, environmental degradation) with benefits (e.g., energy production, job creation).

Application:

Determining the economic viability of renewable vs. non-renewable energy sources.

Assessing affordability and long-term sustainability.

4. Geospatial Tools

GIS and Remote Sensing: Used to map optimal locations for renewable energy projects, considering factors such as sunlight exposure, wind speeds, and proximity to transmission infrastructure.

Drone Technology: Facilitates site surveys and monitoring of construction activities.

5. Social Impact Assessments (SIA)

Focuses on evaluating the impacts of energy projects on local communities, particularly in terms of displacement, access to benefits, and cultural considerations.

6.2.3 Mitigation Measures

1. Promoting Clean Energy Technologies

Adopting Renewables: Transitioning from fossil fuels to renewable energy sources reduces GHG emissions and dependence on finite resources.

Energy Efficiency: Upgrading transmission and distribution systems to reduce energy losses and improve efficiency.

2. Minimizing Land Use Conflicts

Careful Site Selection: Prioritize sites with minimal ecological and social conflicts, such as degraded lands or offshore areas for wind farms.

Compensation and Livelihood Restoration: Provide fair compensation to affected communities and implement programs to restore livelihoods.

3. Biodiversity Protection

Wildlife-Friendly Designs: Use turbine designs that minimize bird and bat collisions; include fish ladders in hydropower projects.

Habitat Restoration: Rehabilitate areas affected by mining or construction activities.

4. Community Benefit-Sharing Mechanisms

Revenue Sharing: Allocate a portion of project revenues to local communities to fund development projects.

Employment Opportunities: Train and hire local workers to ensure that communities benefit from job creation.

6.2.4 Case Studies

1. The Three Gorges Dam, China

Achievements: The world's largest hydropower project generates significant renewable energy and reduces coal consumption.

Challenges: Displacement of over a million people and disruption of aquatic ecosystems highlight the need for comprehensive social and environmental assessments.

2. Solar Power Projects in Rajasthan, India

Achievements: Large-scale solar farms have contributed to India's renewable energy goals, providing clean energy to millions.

Challenges: Land use conflicts and concerns over biodiversity in desert ecosystems emphasize the importance of site selection and mitigation measures.

3. Offshore Wind Farms in Denmark

Achievements: Denmark's wind farms have set global benchmarks for renewable energy adoption and community participation.

Challenges: High initial costs and marine biodiversity impacts underline the need for balanced planning.

Emerging Trends in the Energy Sector

Decentralized Energy Systems: Small-scale, community-based renewable energy projects reduce reliance on centralized grids and empower local communities.

Energy Storage Solutions: Advances in battery technology enable efficient storage of renewable energy, addressing intermittency issues.

Carbon Capture and Storage (CCS): Technologies that capture CO_2 emissions from fossil fuel plants are gaining attention as transitional solutions.

Energy and power projects are indispensable for meeting global energy needs and transitioning to sustainable development. However, their far-reaching impacts require careful planning, assessment, and mitigation. By leveraging advanced tools such as LCA, EIA, and GIS, and implementing community-centric approaches, it is possible to strike a balance between development and sustainability. Renewable energy sources, when coupled with equitable practices and innovative technologies, hold the key to an energy-secure and environmentally responsible future.

6.3 Industrial and Manufacturing Projects

Industrial and manufacturing projects form the cornerstone of economic development, driving growth, innovation, and employment. They are pivotal in transforming raw materials into goods and services that fuel global economies. However, these projects are often linked with significant environmental degradation, social challenges, and economic disparities. A holistic understanding and management of their impacts are essential for sustainable industrialization.

6.3.1 Key Impacts of Industrial and Manufacturing Projects

1. Environmental Impacts

Industrial and manufacturing processes are resource-intensive, contributing to various forms of pollution and environmental stress.

Air Pollution:

Industrial emissions release pollutants such as sulfur dioxide (SO_2), nitrogen oxides (NO_x), volatile organic compounds (VOCs), and particulate matter into the atmosphere.

The burning of fossil fuels in factories contributes significantly to greenhouse gas (GHG) emissions, exacerbating climate change.

Water Pollution:

Discharge of untreated industrial effluents containing heavy metals, chemicals, and toxins into water bodies leads to water contamination and loss of aquatic biodiversity.

Overuse of water resources for industrial cooling or production depletes groundwater and affects community water access.

Hazardous Waste Generation:

Industrial processes produce hazardous byproducts, including chemical residues, e-waste, and medical waste, which require proper disposal to avoid soil and water contamination.

Resource Depletion:

Mining, logging, and extraction of raw materials for manufacturing lead to habitat destruction and depletion of finite natural resources.

Energy-intensive industrial operations further strain the planet's energy resources.

Loss of Biodiversity:

Deforestation and land use changes for establishing industrial facilities often result in habitat fragmentation and loss of biodiversity.

2. Social Impacts

While industrial projects offer numerous economic benefits, they also create social challenges, particularly for workers and nearby communities.

Occupational Health Risks:

Workers are exposed to hazardous chemicals, heavy machinery, and unsafe working conditions, leading to occupational diseases and injuries.

Poor workplace safety standards can result in industrial accidents, with long-term repercussions on employees and their families.

Labor Rights Violations:

Exploitative labor practices, including low wages, long working hours, and lack of job security, are prevalent in some industrial sectors.

Gender-based disparities and discrimination in hiring and wages remain a concern.

Community Disruptions:

The establishment of industrial zones may lead to the displacement of communities and loss of traditional livelihoods.

Industrial pollution can adversely affect the health and well-being of nearby residents, leading to social unrest.

3. Economic Impacts

Despite their environmental and social challenges, industrial projects are crucial for economic development.

Economic Growth:

Industrialization contributes significantly to GDP growth, especially in developing countries transitioning from agrarian economies.

Manufacturing industries support technological innovation and diversification of the economy.

Job Creation:

Industrial projects generate employment opportunities, from unskilled labor to high-tech jobs, promoting socio-economic mobility.

Local Supply Chains:

Establishment of manufacturing facilities often strengthens local supply chains by creating demand for raw materials, transport, and logistics services.

Income Inequality:

While industries generate wealth, disparities in wage distribution and job opportunities may widen the gap between socio-economic groups.

6.3.2 Assessment Tools and Approaches

1. Industrial Risk Assessment

Purpose: Identifies and evaluates potential risks associated with industrial processes, including chemical spills, explosions, and emissions.

Applications:

Development of emergency response plans.

Ensuring compliance with environmental and safety regulations.

Identifying areas for process improvement.

2. Supply Chain Analysis

Purpose: Examines the environmental and social impacts of raw material sourcing, production, and distribution processes.

Applications:

Promoting ethical sourcing of raw materials.

Reducing carbon footprints through optimized supply chain logistics.

Identifying opportunities for circular economy practices.

3. Social Impact Assessments (SIA)

Focus Areas:

Labor conditions and compliance with workplace standards.

Impact of industrial pollution on community health and safety.

Evaluation of community engagement and benefit-sharing practices.

4. Environmental Impact Assessments (EIA)

Applications:

Assessing emissions, waste generation, and resource consumption.

Identifying potential biodiversity impacts of industrial facilities.

Recommending mitigation measures to minimize environmental harm.

6.3.3 Mitigation Measures

1. Cleaner Production Technologies

Adopting technologies that minimize waste and emissions, such as low-carbon manufacturing processes and renewable energy-powered production.

Implementing waste-to-energy systems to recycle industrial byproducts.

2. Waste Minimization Strategies

Promoting the reuse and recycling of materials within industrial processes.

Establishing proper waste management facilities to handle hazardous byproducts.

3. Occupational Health and Safety Standards

Ensuring compliance with international safety standards, such as ISO 45001.

Providing regular health check-ups, protective gear, and training for workers.

4. Community Engagement

Involving local communities in decision-making processes to address their concerns and expectations.

Developing corporate social responsibility (CSR) programs to fund education, healthcare, and infrastructure in nearby areas.

5. Sustainable Resource Management

Using renewable energy sources to power industrial facilities.

Implementing water-saving technologies, such as closed-loop cooling systems and wastewater recycling.

6.3.4 Case Studies

1. Sustainable Manufacturing in the Automotive Sector

Example: Toyota's "Environmental Challenge 2050" aims to reduce CO_2 emissions, promote resource recycling, and develop eco-friendly vehicles.

Lessons: Integration of sustainability goals into industrial operations leads to long-term economic and environmental benefits.

2. Zero Discharge Textile Parks in India

Example: Tamil Nadu's textile parks have adopted zero liquid discharge (ZLD) technology, treating and reusing wastewater within the industry.

Lessons: Proactive environmental measures can mitigate the ecological impacts of water-intensive industries.

3. Community Impact in Oil Refinery Projects

Example: Chevron's refinery project in Nigeria includes extensive CSR initiatives for healthcare, education, and infrastructure.

Lessons: Effective community engagement reduces social conflicts and builds local trust.

Emerging Trends in Industrial Development

Green Manufacturing: Adoption of green technologies and processes to reduce environmental footprints.

Industry 4.0: Integration of smart technologies, such as IoT and AI, for efficient resource utilization and waste reduction.

Circular Economy: Transitioning from a linear "take-make-dispose" model to circular systems emphasizing reuse, repair, and recycling.

Localization of Supply Chains: Strengthening regional supply chains to reduce transport emissions and support local economies.

Industrial and manufacturing projects are vital for socio-economic progress but must be developed and operated responsibly. A balanced approach, incorporating advanced assessment tools, stakeholder engagement, and sustainable practices, can minimize adverse impacts and enhance benefits. By adopting innovative technologies and aligning with global sustainability goals, industrial projects can drive inclusive growth while preserving environmental and social well-being.

6.4 Agriculture and Rural Development

Agriculture and rural development projects are crucial for enhancing food security, alleviating poverty, and driving socio-economic progress in rural areas. These projects address a spectrum of objectives, including increasing agricultural productivity, diversifying livelihoods, and developing rural infrastructure. However, their implementation brings both opportunities and challenges, significantly influencing environmental sustainability, social dynamics, and economic growth.

6.4.1 Key Impacts of Agriculture and Rural Development Projects

1. Environmental Impacts

Agriculture and rural development activities, while essential for sustaining rural economies, often put substantial pressure on natural ecosystems.

Deforestation:

Agricultural expansion, especially for commercial crops, often leads to the clearing of forests, resulting in habitat destruction and biodiversity loss.

Slash-and-burn practices, prevalent in some regions, exacerbate deforestation and soil erosion.

Soil Degradation:

Intensive farming practices can degrade soil health through nutrient depletion, salinization, and compaction.

Overuse of chemical fertilizers and pesticides contaminates soil and reduces its fertility.

Water Overuse:

Excessive irrigation depletes groundwater reserves and can lead to waterlogging and salinity.

Unsustainable water extraction impacts nearby ecosystems and disrupts aquatic biodiversity.

Biodiversity Loss:

Monoculture farming reduces genetic diversity in crops, increasing vulnerability to pests and diseases.

Habitat destruction for farming negatively affects wildlife populations.

Greenhouse Gas Emissions:

Agriculture contributes significantly to methane (from rice paddies and livestock) and nitrous oxide emissions (from fertilizers).

Deforestation and land-use changes release stored carbon, contributing to global warming.

2. Social Impacts

Agriculture and rural development projects can transform the socio-economic fabric of rural areas, influencing equity, social cohesion, and cultural practices.

Livelihood Impacts:

While these projects aim to improve rural incomes, they can displace traditional practices and livelihoods, particularly for marginalized groups like indigenous communities.

Mechanization and modern farming techniques may reduce the demand for manual labor, affecting rural employment.

Gender Dynamics:

Projects that fail to account for gender roles in agriculture may unintentionally marginalize women, who often play a critical role in farming and resource management.

Conversely, gender-sensitive projects can empower women through access to resources, training, and decision-making opportunities.

Access to Resources:

Unequal distribution of project benefits, such as irrigation facilities or financial support, can exacerbate existing inequalities among farmers and landless laborers.

Conflicts over land rights and resource allocation are common in projects that do not involve local stakeholders.

Social Cohesion:

Displacement or significant changes in traditional practices can disrupt social harmony.

Participatory approaches that involve communities in project planning and implementation enhance trust and cohesion.

3. Economic Impacts

Agriculture and rural development projects have far-reaching economic implications, influencing both local and national economies.

Rural Economy Stimulation:

By improving productivity and diversifying income sources, these projects stimulate rural economies, creating new markets and employment opportunities.

Enhanced connectivity through rural infrastructure boosts trade and access to urban markets.

Food Security:

Increased agricultural output contributes to food availability and affordability, addressing malnutrition and hunger.

Diversification into high-value crops and livestock improves dietary diversity and income stability.

Agricultural Productivity:

Investments in modern farming techniques, irrigation, and storage facilities enhance crop yields and reduce post-harvest losses.

Access to credit and training enables farmers to adopt innovative practices.

Market Integration:

Infrastructure development, such as roads and cold storage, facilitates the integration of rural producers into national and global supply chains.

6.4.2 Assessment Tools and Approaches

To maximize the benefits and minimize adverse effects, various tools and approaches are employed to assess the impacts of agriculture and rural development projects.

1. Water and Soil Quality Monitoring

Regular monitoring of water and soil parameters ensures sustainable use of these resources.

Techniques such as soil testing, remote sensing, and groundwater mapping provide insights into resource health and project impacts.

2. Livelihood Assessments

These assessments analyze the effects of projects on rural incomes, employment, and household well-being.

They identify vulnerable groups and recommend interventions to ensure equitable benefits.

3. Participatory Rural Appraisal (PRA)

PRA involves local communities in assessing their needs, resources, and potential project impacts.

This approach ensures that projects align with local priorities and cultural practices.

4. Environmental Impact Assessments (EIA)

EIAs evaluate the potential environmental consequences of agricultural projects, focusing on land use, water resources, and biodiversity.

Recommendations from EIAs guide the adoption of mitigation measures.

5. Gender Analysis

Gender analysis identifies the roles, responsibilities, and needs of men and women in agriculture.

It informs the design of gender-sensitive interventions to promote equality and empowerment.

6.4.3 Mitigation Measures

Effective mitigation strategies are essential to address the environmental, social, and economic challenges associated with agriculture and rural development projects.

1. Promoting Sustainable Agricultural Practices

Crop Rotation and Diversification:

Alternating crops reduces pest and disease cycles, improves soil health, and enhances resilience to climate change.

Organic Farming:

Reducing chemical inputs improves soil and water quality while fetching premium prices in markets.

Conservation Agriculture:

Techniques such as minimum tillage and cover cropping maintain soil integrity and moisture.

2. Improving Rural Infrastructure

Irrigation Systems:

Efficient irrigation methods, such as drip and sprinkler systems, conserve water and enhance productivity.

Storage and Processing Facilities:

Investments in cold storage and food processing reduce post-harvest losses and add value to agricultural produce.

Rural Roads:

Improved connectivity reduces transportation costs and enhances access to markets and services.

3. Ensuring Equitable Access

Targeted Support for Marginalized Groups:

Providing subsidies, training, and credit facilities to smallholders and landless farmers ensures inclusive growth.

Community Benefit-Sharing:

Engaging local communities in project design and profit-sharing enhances their ownership and well-being.

4. Conserving Natural Resources

Integrated Water Resource Management (IWRM):

Coordinated management of water, land, and related resources ensures sustainable usage.

Afforestation and Agroforestry:

Planting trees alongside crops restores ecosystems and provides additional income sources.

Soil Conservation Measures:

Techniques like contour farming and terracing prevent soil erosion in hilly areas.

6.4.4 Case Studies

1. Sustainable Agriculture in Andhra Pradesh, India

Initiative: Zero Budget Natural Farming (ZBNF) promotes chemical-free farming techniques.

Impact:

Improved soil fertility and water conservation.

Reduced input costs for farmers, leading to higher incomes.

2. Rural Development in Ethiopia

Initiative: The Productive Safety Net Program (PSNP) focuses on food security through public works and livelihood support.

Impact:

Enhanced household resilience to food insecurity.

Improved rural infrastructure and agricultural productivity.

3. Integrated Watershed Management in Kenya

Initiative: Community-led watershed management projects for water conservation and reforestation.

Impact:

Increased water availability for irrigation and drinking.

Enhanced biodiversity and reduced soil erosion.

Agriculture and rural development projects are instrumental in addressing critical global challenges such as hunger, poverty, and environmental degradation. By integrating sustainable practices, participatory approaches, and equitable benefit-sharing, these projects can transform rural areas into hubs of resilience and prosperity. Effective planning and impact assessment are essential to maximize their benefits while minimizing adverse effects, ensuring long-term sustainability and inclusivity.

6.5 Urban Development and Smart Cities

Urban development and smart city initiatives are at the forefront of global efforts to address rapid urbanization, enhance quality of life, and create sustainable urban environments. By combining innovative technologies, sustainable infrastructure, and efficient service delivery, these projects aim to tackle challenges such as overcrowding, environmental degradation, and social inequity.

6.5.1 Key Impacts of Urban Development and Smart City Initiatives

1. Environmental Impacts

Urban development and smart city projects have significant environmental implications, often requiring careful planning to ensure sustainability.

Loss of Green Spaces:

Urban sprawl often results in the conversion of green areas into residential, commercial, or industrial zones.

The reduction in vegetation affects biodiversity and urban ecosystems, exacerbating the urban heat island effect.

Increased Energy Consumption:

Expanding urban infrastructure and growing populations increase the demand for energy, often straining existing resources.

Inefficient energy use in buildings, transportation, and industrial sectors contributes to greenhouse gas emissions.

Waste Generation:

Urban areas generate substantial amounts of solid waste, electronic waste, and wastewater.

Improper waste management leads to environmental pollution, health risks, and resource depletion.

Air and Water Pollution:

Emissions from vehicles, industries, and construction activities degrade air quality.

Urban runoff and untreated sewage contaminate water bodies, affecting aquatic ecosystems and public health.

2. Social Impacts

Urban development and smart city projects influence social dynamics in multiple ways, often yielding both positive and negative outcomes.

Improved Access to Services:

Enhanced infrastructure ensures better access to housing, healthcare, education, and public transportation.

Technological innovations improve service delivery and responsiveness, particularly in sectors like healthcare and emergency management.

Gentrification and Displacement:

Urban renewal projects and rising property values often displace low-income populations, leading to social stratification.

Displacement can disrupt communities, livelihoods, and access to affordable housing and essential services.

Enhanced Safety and Security:

Smart city technologies such as surveillance systems and predictive analytics improve public safety and crime prevention.

However, excessive surveillance may raise concerns about privacy and data security.

Social Inclusion and Equity:

Urban development can reduce inequalities by providing inclusive services, but poorly planned projects may widen disparities.

Addressing the needs of marginalized groups, such as the urban poor and disabled, is critical for achieving equitable outcomes.

3. Economic Impacts

Urban development and smart city projects are key drivers of economic growth, attracting investments and generating employment.

Boosting Urban Economies:

Investments in smart infrastructure, technology hubs, and real estate stimulate economic activities and increase city revenues.

The integration of technology creates opportunities in sectors like IT, telecommunications, and green energy.

Job Creation:

Construction, operation, and maintenance of urban infrastructure generate employment across various skill levels.

Smart cities create high-tech jobs in data analysis, urban planning, and energy management.

Attracting Investments:

Well-planned urban areas with efficient infrastructure attract domestic and foreign investments.

Smart cities are seen as hubs of innovation, fostering startups and entrepreneurship.

Rising Living Costs:

Economic growth often raises the cost of living, particularly in housing, utilities, and transportation.

Balancing economic opportunities with affordability is essential for sustainable urban development.

6.5.2 Assessment Tools and Approaches

To evaluate the impacts of urban development and smart city projects, a range of assessment tools and approaches are utilized. These tools help in planning, monitoring, and ensuring the sustainability of urban initiatives.

1. Urban Sustainability Indicators

Indicators measure progress in key areas such as air quality, water management, energy efficiency, and waste reduction.

Examples include the Sustainable Development Goals (SDGs) related to urban development, such as SDG 11 (Sustainable Cities and Communities).

2. Social Equity Assessments

These assessments examine the inclusivity, affordability, and accessibility of urban projects.

They focus on the impacts on marginalized groups, including low-income populations, minorities, and persons with disabilities.

3. Big Data Analytics

Real-time data from sensors, mobile apps, and IoT devices monitor traffic flow, energy usage, waste management, and public service delivery.

Predictive analytics help identify patterns and optimize resource allocation.

4. Environmental Impact Assessments (EIA)

EIAs evaluate the potential environmental consequences of urban projects, identifying mitigation measures for issues such as pollution and biodiversity loss.

Cumulative impact assessments consider the combined effects of multiple projects in an urban area.

5. Public Participation Tools

Tools such as community workshops, surveys, and participatory mapping involve residents in urban planning and decision-making.

This approach ensures that projects reflect local needs and priorities.

6.5.3 Mitigation Measures

Mitigation strategies aim to address the environmental, social, and economic challenges posed by urban development and smart city projects, ensuring sustainable and equitable outcomes.

1. Integrating Green Infrastructure

Incorporating green building standards, rooftop gardens, and vertical forests reduces energy consumption and enhances air quality.

Urban parks and green corridors mitigate the urban heat island effect and provide recreational spaces.

2. Promoting Renewable Energy

Smart cities can transition to renewable energy sources such as solar, wind, and biomass for power generation.

Implementing energy-efficient technologies in buildings and public transportation reduces dependency on fossil fuels.

3. Developing Affordable Housing

Mixed-income housing developments ensure that low-income populations have access to affordable living spaces.

Housing policies should include rent control measures and incentives for developers to provide affordable units.

4. Expanding Public Transportation

Investments in metro systems, electric buses, and bike-sharing programs reduce traffic congestion and emissions.

Accessible and affordable public transportation promotes inclusivity and mobility for all residents.

5. Waste Management Innovations

Smart waste bins with sensors can monitor fill levels and optimize collection routes.

Promoting recycling, composting, and waste-to-energy technologies minimizes landfill use and resource wastage.

6. Engaging Communities

Community engagement fosters a sense of ownership and trust among residents, enhancing project acceptance.

Transparent communication and grievance redress mechanisms ensure that all stakeholders have a voice.

6.5.4 Case Studies

1. Singapore's Smart Nation Initiative

Singapore's Smart Nation program focuses on leveraging technology to improve urban living and governance.

Key Features:

Real-time traffic management and electronic road pricing.

Smart housing with energy-efficient appliances and IoT integration.

Digital healthcare solutions for elderly care.

Impacts:

Enhanced efficiency and sustainability in urban systems.

Improved quality of life for residents.

2. Curitiba, Brazil

Curitiba's integrated urban planning focuses on sustainable development through green infrastructure and public transport.

Key Features:

Bus Rapid Transit (BRT) system for efficient and affordable transportation.

Urban parks and green belts to manage floods and improve air quality.

Impacts:

Reduced vehicular emissions and traffic congestion.

Enhanced urban resilience to environmental challenges.

3. India's Smart Cities Mission

The mission aims to develop 100 smart cities focusing on core infrastructure, technology, and citizen services.

Key Features:

Smart governance through e-governance platforms.

Renewable energy projects and waste management systems.

Impacts:

Improved service delivery and urban livability.

Increased investments in infrastructure and technology.

Urban development and smart city initiatives are pivotal in addressing the challenges of modern urbanization. By integrating sustainable practices, leveraging technology, and fostering inclusivity, these projects can transform cities into hubs of innovation, resilience, and equity. A balanced approach that considers environmental sustainability, social justice, and economic growth is essential to ensure that these initiatives benefit all stakeholders while safeguarding the planet for future generations.

6.6 Water, Sanitation, and Waste Management Projects

Water, sanitation, and waste management projects are essential components of sustainable development, contributing significantly to public health, environmental sustainability, and urban resilience. These projects address critical issues such as access to clean drinking water, improved sanitation facilities, and efficient waste disposal systems, all of which are vital for enhancing quality of life and achieving the United Nations' Sustainable Development Goals (SDGs).

6.6.1 Key Impacts of Water, Sanitation, and Waste Management Projects

1. Environmental Impacts

Water, sanitation, and waste management projects have profound environmental implications, both positive and negative.

Impact on Water Resources:

Large-scale water infrastructure projects, such as dams and reservoirs, can alter natural water flows, affect aquatic ecosystems, and reduce water availability downstream.

Poorly managed wastewater systems contribute to water pollution, impacting biodiversity and human health.

Waste Generation and Pollution:

Solid waste management projects influence the amount and type of waste reaching landfills or open dumps. Improperly managed waste can lead to soil and groundwater contamination.

Construction of new facilities for waste and wastewater treatment can have short-term environmental impacts such as land use changes and emissions.

Climate Implications:

Methane emissions from unmanaged waste and open dumps are a

significant contributor to greenhouse gases.

Energy-intensive water and sanitation projects, such as desalination, may increase carbon footprints if powered by fossil fuels.

2. Social Impacts

Water, sanitation, and waste management projects have transformative effects on social well-being.

Improved Health Outcomes:

Access to clean water and sanitation reduces the prevalence of waterborne diseases such as cholera and diarrhea.

Proper waste management decreases vector-borne diseases like malaria and dengue.

Gender Empowerment:

Women and girls benefit significantly from improved water and sanitation facilities, reducing the time spent fetching water and ensuring privacy and safety.

Sanitation projects in schools improve attendance and educational outcomes, especially for girls.

Support for Livelihoods:

Projects often generate employment opportunities, particularly in waste collection, recycling, and facility operations.

Community-based approaches can empower local populations and promote social cohesion.

Challenges of Displacement and Equity:

Large-scale water projects, such as dams, may displace communities, impacting their livelihoods and cultural heritage.

Ensuring equitable access to services in urban and rural areas remains a persistent challenge.

3. Economic Impacts

Cost Savings and Productivity Gains:

Improved sanitation and water services reduce healthcare costs by preventing diseases.

Better waste management systems reduce environmental cleanup costs and support recycling industries.

Barriers to Implementation:

High capital investment for water treatment plants, sewage systems, and modern waste management facilities can strain public budgets.

Operation and maintenance costs may pose long-term financial challenges, particularly in low-income regions.

Economic Opportunities:

Waste management initiatives create opportunities in recycling, composting, and waste-to-energy sectors.

Reliable water and sanitation systems attract businesses and industries, boosting local economies.

6.6.2 Assessment Tools and Approaches

The effective planning and implementation of water, sanitation, and waste management projects rely on various assessment tools and methodologies to evaluate their impacts.

1. Hydrological Models

These models simulate water flows, availability, and quality, helping to predict the impacts of water projects on local and regional hydrology.

They are crucial for assessing the sustainability of water extraction, impacts of dams, and potential risks of flooding or drought.

2. Public Health Indicators

Public health data is used to measure improvements in hygiene, disease reduction, and overall well-being attributable to water and sanitation interventions.

Indicators include reduced incidences of waterborne diseases and increased access to safe drinking water.

3. Waste Audits

Waste audits assess the quantity and composition of waste generated in a given area.

They help design effective waste management systems by identifying recycling and waste-to-energy opportunities.

4. Environmental Impact Assessments (EIAs)

EIAs evaluate the potential environmental consequences of projects, ensuring compliance with environmental standards and identifying mitigation measures.

5. Social Impact Assessments (SIAs)

SIAs examine the effects of projects on communities, focusing on displacement, access to services, and equitable benefit-sharing.

6.6.2 Mitigation Measures

To ensure sustainable and inclusive outcomes, water, sanitation, and waste management projects incorporate a range of mitigation measures.

1. Adopting Circular Economy Principles in Waste Management

Transitioning from linear waste systems to circular models reduces resource consumption and waste generation.

Practices include promoting recycling, composting organic waste, and designing products for reuse.

2. Promoting Community-Based Water and Sanitation Solutions

Engaging local communities in the design and implementation of projects ensures that solutions are tailored to specific needs.

Community-led approaches often lead to better maintenance and higher acceptance of systems.

3. Investing in Modern Wastewater Treatment Technologies

Advanced treatment technologies such as membrane filtration and anaerobic digestion improve wastewater quality and enable resource recovery.

Decentralized systems are particularly effective in rural or low-density urban areas, where centralized systems may be impractical.

4. Integrating Green Infrastructure

Green infrastructure solutions, such as wetlands for wastewater treatment and urban rain gardens, provide cost-effective and environmentally friendly alternatives.

These systems enhance biodiversity, improve water quality, and reduce urban heat.

5. Strengthening Policy and Regulation

Comprehensive policies that mandate waste segregation, recycling, and treatment incentivize sustainable practices.

Clear regulatory frameworks for water use, sanitation standards, and waste management ensure compliance and accountability.

6. Leveraging Technology and Innovation

IoT-enabled systems for water quality monitoring and smart waste bins with fill-level sensors improve efficiency.

Mobile apps for citizen reporting of waste issues and water service disruptions enhance transparency and responsiveness.

6.6.3 Case Studies

1. Clean India Mission (Swachh Bharat Abhiyan), India

This initiative aims to eliminate open defecation and improve waste management across the country.

Key Features:

Construction of millions of toilets in rural and urban areas.

Awareness campaigns promoting behavioral change.

Focus on solid waste management, including segregation and recycling.

Impacts:

Significant reduction in open defecation and associated diseases.

Improved cleanliness and hygiene in public spaces.

2. Stockholm's Waste-to-Energy Program

Stockholm is a global leader in waste management, with nearly 99% of waste being recycled or used for energy recovery.

Key Features:

Advanced waste-to-energy plants convert non-recyclable waste into heat and electricity.

Stringent recycling regulations ensure high participation rates.

Impacts:

Reduced reliance on landfills.

Increased energy security and greenhouse gas reduction.

3. Manila Water Company, Philippines

The company provides water and wastewater services to Metro Manila, focusing on sustainability and inclusivity.

Key Features:

Innovative technologies for water treatment and distribution.

Community engagement programs for underserved areas.

Impacts:

Improved access to clean water for low-income communities.

Enhanced wastewater treatment capacity.

Conclusion

Sector-specific impact assessments are critical tools that provide customized frameworks to address the distinct challenges and opportunities associated with projects across diverse sectors such as energy, infrastructure, agriculture, and urban development. By systematically evaluating environmental, social, and economic impacts, these assessments ensure a balanced and holistic approach to decision-making, promoting sustainability, equity, and long-term effectiveness. They enable the identification of potential risks and benefits, guiding the implementation of mitigation and enhancement measures that align with broader development goals. Collaborative engagement among stakeholders fosters inclusivity and accountability, while adaptive management ensures responsiveness to evolving conditions and unforeseen challenges. Additionally, the integration of innovative tools and technologies, such as GIS, big data analytics, and green solutions, enhances precision and efficiency in planning and execution. Ultimately, these assessments are indispensable for maximizing project benefits, minimizing harm, and ensuring that development initiatives contribute positively to society and the environment.

CHAPTER VII

Data Gaps and Limitations in Impact Assessment

Impact assessment is an essential tool for evaluating the potential consequences of a project on the environment, society, and economy. However, despite its importance, there are several challenges and limitations in the impact assessment process that can undermine its effectiveness and accuracy. These challenges range from data gaps and uncertainty in impact prediction to stakeholder resistance, institutional barriers, and difficulties in monitoring and evaluating outcomes. This chapter will delve into these challenges, analyzing their impact on the assessment process and exploring potential solutions to address them.

7.1 Data Gaps and Uncertainty in Impact Prediction

7.1.1 Overview of Data Gaps in Impact Assessment

One of the foremost challenges in conducting effective impact assessments is the lack of comprehensive, reliable, and current data. Accurate impact prediction depends on having access to robust baseline data and predictive models that can forecast the potential effects of a project. However, gaps in data can lead to incomplete or misleading assessments.

I) Lack of Baseline Data:

Baseline data is crucial for comparing the conditions before and after a project. In many instances, baseline data on environmental, social, and economic conditions is either unavailable or of low quality. This makes it difficult to evaluate the true magnitude of a project's impact. For example, in rural areas, the lack of historical data on soil quality, water resources, and biodiversity can hinder the assessment of environmental risks posed by a new agricultural or industrial project.

II) Insufficient Data Collection:

In some cases, data collection is limited to a narrow set of indicators, failing to capture the full scope of potential impacts. This might be due to time constraints, budget limitations, or the difficulty of gathering data in remote or underserved areas. For example, air quality monitoring may focus only on particulate matter but ignore volatile organic compounds that also have significant health impacts.

III) Lack of Local Knowledge:

Many projects, especially in rural or indigenous areas, require local knowledge for effective impact assessment. However, traditional ecological knowledge (TEK) is often undervalued in formal assessments. The lack of integration of local knowledge into the impact assessment process can result in the overlooking of critical environmental or social issues.

IV) Uncertainty in Predicting Impacts

Impact predictions, particularly for long-term or large-scale projects, are often based on models that rely on assumptions. These assumptions, combined with incomplete data, introduce a degree of uncertainty into impact assessments.

V) Environmental Uncertainty:

Predicting the long-term environmental impacts of a project, such as the effects of deforestation on biodiversity or climate change, is inherently uncertain. Climate models, for example, have limitations in predicting regional changes in precipitation or temperature, making it difficult to estimate how an infrastructure project will interact with future environmental conditions.

VI) Social and Economic Uncertainty:

Social and economic predictions are equally fraught with uncertainty. Predicting the impacts on community well-being, income levels, or migration patterns can be especially difficult, as these factors are influenced by a wide range of external variables. Social dynamics such as migration trends, political stability, and market fluctuations can dramatically affect project outcomes, yet these are challenging to quantify or predict with high confidence.

VII) Scenario-Based Uncertainty:

Many impact assessments rely on different scenarios (best-case, worst-case, and most likely scenarios) to account for uncertainties. However, the inherent subjectivity in selecting these scenarios introduces uncertainty in the evaluation process.

7.1.2 Solutions for Addressing Data Gaps and Uncertainty

I) Improved Data Collection and Monitoring:

Implementing more robust data collection methodologies, including remote sensing, real-time monitoring systems, and community-based data collection, can help address data gaps.

II) Integration of Local Knowledge:

Incorporating local or indigenous knowledge can help fill in data gaps and provide a more accurate understanding of the local environment and social conditions. This approach also fosters better community engagement.

III) Adaptive Management:

An adaptive management approach, where the project is continuously monitored and adjustments are made based on evolving conditions, can help mitigate uncertainty. This requires flexibility and responsiveness from both project planners and stakeholders.

7.2 Stakeholder Resistance and Conflicts

7.2.1 Overview of Stakeholder Resistance

Stakeholder resistance to projects is a common challenge in impact assessments. Resistance can stem from a variety of sources, including local communities, environmental groups, and even internal stakeholders within the organization overseeing the project. These conflicts may arise due to perceived threats to local livelihoods, cultural heritage, environmental quality, or social equity.

I) Community Resistance:

Local communities, particularly in rural and indigenous areas, may resist projects that threaten their land, resources, or way of life. For example, a mining project in a rural area may face resistance from local farmers who fear the loss of fertile land, access to water, or the disruption of their traditional lifestyle. Similarly, large infrastructure projects such as dams or highways can displace communities, leading to protests and legal challenges.

II) Environmental Activism:

Environmental organizations may oppose projects that they perceive as harmful to the environment. For instance, large-scale industrial projects or energy developments such as coal plants or oil drilling operations often attract protests due to concerns over air pollution, water contamination, and habitat destruction.

III) Political and Economic Interests:

Political and economic actors may resist projects for reasons unrelated to environmental or social considerations, such as political favoritism, economic power dynamics, or vested interests in maintaining the status quo. Political elites may resist projects that challenge their control over resources, and local elites may oppose projects that threaten their economic dominance.

7.2.2 Resolving Stakeholder Conflicts

I) Early Stakeholder Engagement:

Proactively engaging stakeholders early in the planning process, ensuring their concerns are heard, and addressing them in the design of the project can reduce resistance and facilitate smoother implementation.

II) Mediation and Conflict Resolution:

Conflict resolution mechanisms, including third-party mediators, can help resolve disputes between stakeholders. Creating a transparent grievance redressal mechanism can help build trust among affected communities.

III) Benefit Sharing:

Offering compensatory benefits, such as job creation, infrastructure improvements, or direct financial compensation, can help mitigate opposition. Transparent and fair benefit-sharing arrangements can reduce resistance, especially when communities perceive tangible benefits from the project.

7.3 Institutional and Regulatory Barriers

7.3.1 Overview of Institutional Challenges

Institutions and regulatory frameworks are often a critical part of the impact assessment process. However, weak institutional capacity, lack of coordination, and inadequate regulatory frameworks can undermine the effectiveness of impact assessments.

I) Lack of Institutional Capacity:

In many developing countries, institutions responsible for environmental and social governance may lack the technical capacity to conduct comprehensive impact assessments. This includes a shortage of skilled personnel, inadequate resources, and a lack of proper tools or methodologies.

II) Regulatory Gaps and Weak Enforcement:

The absence of clear regulations or poorly enforced laws can lead to ineffective impact assessments. For example, in some countries, environmental regulations may not be updated to reflect current scientific knowledge, leading to outdated or insufficient assessment practices.

III) Coordination Failures:

Impact assessments often involve multiple agencies, such as environmental ministries, social development agencies, and local governments. Poor coordination among these agencies can result in delays, conflicting priorities, and fragmented assessments that fail to address the full range of project impacts.

7.3.2 Solutions for Addressing Institutional and Regulatory Barriers

I) Strengthening Institutional Capacity:

Building the technical capacity of institutions responsible for impact assessments is essential. This includes investing in training, technology, and resources to improve the quality and efficiency of assessments.

II) Regulatory Reforms:

Updating and harmonizing environmental and social regulations to reflect modern challenges can improve the quality of impact assessments. Governments can also create clearer guidelines on how to assess cumulative impacts and long-term sustainability.

III) Enhanced Inter-Institutional Coordination:

Establishing clear roles and responsibilities for all stakeholders involved in impact assessments can reduce conflicts and inefficiencies. Regular communication and joint decision-making processes can enhance coordination.

7.4 Challenges in Monitoring and Evaluation

7.4.1 Overview of Monitoring and Evaluation Challenges

Monitoring and evaluation (M&E) are critical for assessing the success of mitigation measures and ensuring that project impacts are managed effectively. However, M&E faces several challenges, particularly in the context of large-scale infrastructure and development projects.

I) Insufficient Monitoring Systems:

Often, the monitoring systems in place are inadequate or non-existent. This can be due to a lack of funding, lack of trained personnel, or insufficient infrastructure for data collection and analysis.

II) Complexity of Long-Term Monitoring:

Monitoring long-term impacts, especially those related to social dynamics, biodiversity, and climate change, can be complex and expensive. Projects may also change over time, leading to evolving impacts that are difficult to track.

III) Data Integrity and Accessibility:

In some cases, monitoring data is incomplete, inconsistent, or inaccessible to key stakeholders. This can result in delays in addressing unforeseen impacts and prevent stakeholders from holding project developers accountable.

7.4.2 Solutions for Addressing Monitoring and Evaluation Challenges

I) Integrated Monitoring Frameworks:

Establishing comprehensive monitoring frameworks that integrate environmental, social, and economic indicators ensures that the full scope of project impacts is tracked. Leveraging technologies like remote sensing and mobile data collection can improve data accuracy and accessibility.

II) Stakeholder Involvement in Monitoring:

Involving local communities and stakeholders in the monitoring process ensures that data is accurate and reflective of local realities. Community-driven monitoring can also enhance accountability and transparency.

III) Adaptive Management and Regular Audits:

Adaptive management, where monitoring results lead to continuous adjustments in project implementation, is essential. Regular audits of both project progress and mitigation effectiveness can help ensure that the project stays on track and delivers its intended outcomes.

Impact assessments are a critical part of project planning and implementation, but they face several challenges. Data gaps, uncertainty in predicting impacts, stakeholder resistance, institutional and regulatory barriers, and difficulties in monitoring and evaluation all limit the effectiveness of impact assessments. By addressing these challenges through improved data collection, stakeholder engagement, institutional strengthening, and robust monitoring systems, we can enhance the accuracy and success of impact assessments, leading to more sustainable and equitable development outcomes.

CHAPTER VIII

Emerging Trends and Innovations in Impact Assessment

Impact assessment has evolved significantly over the past few decades, from a primarily regulatory tool to a comprehensive approach that supports sustainable development, accountability, and better decision-making. As environmental, social, and economic challenges become more complex, the need for innovative methods and technologies to assess, predict, and monitor project impacts has never been greater. This chapter will explore emerging trends and innovations that are reshaping the landscape of impact assessments, focusing on the roles of Artificial Intelligence (AI) and Big Data, climate change and disaster risk assessments, gender and social inclusion, the integration of ESG frameworks, and the use of digital tools and platforms for real-time monitoring.

8.1 Role of Artificial Intelligence and Big Data in Impact Assessment

8.1.1 The Evolution of AI and Big Data in Impact Assessment

The advent of Artificial Intelligence (AI) and Big Data has transformed many industries, including impact assessment. The ability to process vast amounts of data, identify patterns, and generate predictions has opened up new possibilities for evaluating project impacts across environmental, social, and economic domains. AI and Big Data tools can provide more accurate, timely, and cost-effective impact assessments, enabling decision-makers to make better-informed choices.

I) AI for Predictive Analytics

AI's ability to process and analyze large datasets allows for more accurate predictive models. These models can forecast the environmental, social, and economic impacts of a project before it is implemented, reducing uncertainty and risk. For example, machine learning algorithms can analyze historical data to predict the future environmental impacts of urbanization, deforestation, or industrial activities, enabling more precise mitigation strategies.

II) Big Data in Monitoring and Evaluation

Big Data allows for the continuous collection of real-time data from various sources, such as sensors, satellites, and social media platforms. By analyzing this data, stakeholders can track the progress of a project in real-time and adjust plans based on emerging trends. In the context of environmental assessments, this means being able to monitor pollution levels, water quality, or biodiversity impacts instantaneously, rather than relying on periodic surveys or reports.

III) Automation and Efficiency

AI can automate repetitive tasks in impact assessments, such as data collection, data cleaning, and the generation of preliminary reports. This reduces human error and frees up time for more complex analysis and decision-making. For example, AI-powered systems can quickly process satellite images to assess land-use changes or deforestation, speeding up the overall impact assessment process.

IV) Data-Driven Decision Making

With Big Data, impact assessments can move from being based on anecdotal evidence to relying on comprehensive, data-driven insights. For instance, social media analytics and geospatial data can provide valuable information about public sentiment, local concerns, and community reactions, which are critical for understanding social impacts.

V) Challenges and Considerations

While AI and Big Data offer numerous benefits, their integration into impact assessments is not without challenges. Issues such as data privacy, the need for specialized skills, and the accuracy of data sources must be carefully managed. Additionally, there is a risk of over-reliance on technology, which could overlook important qualitative aspects of impact that may not be captured through quantitative data alone.

8.2 Climate Change and Disaster Risk Assessments

8.2.1 Impact of Climate Change on Impact Assessments

Climate change is one of the most pressing global challenges, and its impacts must be integrated into all forms of impact assessments. As climate-related risks become more severe and widespread, climate change and disaster risk assessments have become integral components of project planning and evaluation.

I) Incorporating Climate Change into Environmental Assessments

Traditional environmental impact assessments often focus on immediate environmental impacts, such as land degradation, water pollution, and habitat destruction. However, climate change introduces long-term, systemic risks that must be considered. For example, a highway project in a coastal area might require additional assessments of sea-level rise, increased flooding, and more extreme weather events. Failure to include climate change projections in environmental impact assessments can lead to poorly designed projects that are vulnerable to future climate risks.

II) Disaster Risk Assessments

Disaster risk assessments are closely related to climate change assessments and are increasingly used to predict and manage the risks posed by natural disasters. These assessments evaluate the potential for disasters, such as floods, droughts, earthquakes, and cyclones, and examine their potential impacts on infrastructure, human settlements, and ecosystems. Incorporating disaster risk assessments into impact evaluations can help reduce the vulnerability of projects and communities to climate-related disasters.

8.2.2 Tools for Climate Change Impact Assessments

Several tools and methodologies have emerged to integrate climate change into impact assessments. These include:

I) Climate Resilience Assessments: Evaluate how projects can adapt to future climate conditions.

II) Vulnerability Mapping: Identifies areas most at risk from climate change.

III) Scenario Planning: Uses different climate change scenarios to assess how projects might fare under varying conditions.

IV) Integration of Climate Change Mitigation and Adaptation Strategies

In addition to assessing climate change risks, impact assessments increasingly incorporate strategies for mitigating greenhouse gas emissions and adapting to climate change. This includes:

V) Sustainable Design and Infrastructure: Designing buildings, roads, and other infrastructure to be resilient to climate impacts.

VI) Carbon Footprint Analysis: Assessing the carbon emissions associated with a project and identifying ways to reduce them.

VII) Climate Adaptation Plans: Identifying measures to adapt to the changing climate, such as improving flood defenses or adopting drought-resistant agricultural practices.

VIII) Challenges and Limitations:Despite the importance of climate change in impact assessments, there are still challenges in incorporating climate data into assessments. Climate models are not always reliable at the local level, and there is often uncertainty regarding future climate scenarios. Additionally, financial and technical limitations may prevent the integration of climate change considerations into impact assessments in low- and middle-income countries.

8.3 Gender and Social Inclusion in Impact Assessments
8.3.1 The Growing Focus on Gender and Social Equity
Gender and social inclusion have become key areas of focus in impact assessments as the understanding of social equity has evolved. Traditionally, impact assessments focused mainly on environmental and economic factors, but increasingly, the importance of understanding and addressing gender dynamics, social inclusion, and inequality is recognized.

I) Gender-Responsive Impact Assessment
Gender-responsive impact assessments aim to analyze how projects affect men, women, and gender minorities differently. They recognize that women and men often experience development outcomes in distinct ways due to differences in roles, responsibilities, and access to resources. For example, a rural infrastructure project might increase access to markets for men while reducing the time burden on women for collecting water.

II) Social Inclusion and Marginalized Groups
Beyond gender, social inclusion addresses the needs of marginalized groups, such as ethnic minorities, persons with disabilities, and low-income communities. An inclusive impact assessment takes into account the differential impacts that a project may have on these groups and ensures that their needs and concerns are addressed. This involves not only assessing impacts but also involving marginalized groups in the decision-making process, ensuring that their voices are heard.

8.3.2 Tools for Gender and Social Inclusion Assessment
Several tools and frameworks have been developed to assess gender and social inclusion in impact assessments:
I) Gender Analysis Frameworks: Tools to identify and analyze gender-specific impacts and opportunities.
II) Social Impact Assessments (SIA): Focuses on the effects of projects on social relationships, structures, and equity.
III) Inclusive Decision-Making Processes: Ensures that marginalized and underrepresented groups are involved in the consultation and decision-making process.
IV) Integrating Gender and Inclusion into Policy and Practice: Effective integration of gender and social inclusion into impact assessments requires a shift in both policy and practice. Policies must be designed to ensure that gender and inclusion are central to the development process, while practitioners need to adopt tools and approaches that actively promote equity and inclusion.

V) Challenges in Gender and Social Inclusion Assessment:The assessment of gender and social inclusion is not without challenges. These include the difficulty of collecting sex-disaggregated data, cultural barriers to addressing gender inequality, and the tendency to overlook informal or unpaid work. Additionally, traditional gender roles and power dynamics may prevent marginalized groups from being fully included in the impact assessment process.

8.4 Integration of ESG (Environmental, Social, and Governance) Frameworks

8.4.1 The Rise of ESG in Impact Assessments

The integration of Environmental, Social, and Governance (ESG) factors into impact assessments has become a significant trend in recent years. ESG criteria are used to evaluate a project's performance in terms of sustainability, ethical governance, and social responsibility. Investors, regulators, and stakeholders are increasingly demanding that projects not only deliver financial returns but also contribute positively to environmental and social outcomes.

I) Environmental Sustainability

Projects that prioritize environmental sustainability reduce their carbon footprint, minimize waste, and protect ecosystems. ESG frameworks in impact assessments ensure that environmental impacts are carefully considered and mitigated, helping projects align with global sustainability goals.

II) Social Responsibility

Social factors in ESG assessments include human rights, community welfare, employee welfare, and public health. A project's social performance is evaluated based on its impact on local communities, including labor practices, human rights, and social equity. For example, a mining project might be assessed for its impact on local communities, workers' rights, and the social infrastructure of the area.

III) Governance and Transparency

Governance refers to the way in which projects are managed, including transparency, accountability, and ethical decision-making. Impact assessments that integrate governance criteria examine whether projects are conducted in a way that is transparent and adheres to principles of good governance, such as fairness, stakeholder engagement, and anti-corruption measures.

8.4.2 The Role of ESG in Sustainable Development

ESG frameworks help ensure that projects are aligned with broader sustainable development goals (SDGs). By integrating ESG criteria into impact assessments, projects can contribute to global goals such as poverty reduction, gender equality, climate action, and economic growth.

I) Challenges in ESG Integration

Despite its potential, the integration of ESG factors into impact assessments faces challenges. These include the lack of standardized ESG metrics, the difficulty of measuring intangible social and governance factors, and the need for capacity-building in assessing governance and social issues.

8.5 Digital Tools and Platforms for Real-Time Impact Monitoring

8.5.1 The Role of Digital Tools in Enhancing Impact Monitoring

Digital tools and platforms have revolutionized the way in which impact assessments are monitored and evaluated. Real-time impact monitoring is now possible through the use of mobile technologies, cloud-based platforms, geospatial systems, and remote sensing technologies.

I) Remote Sensing and Geospatial Technologies

Geospatial tools, such as Geographic Information Systems (GIS) and remote sensing technologies (e.g., satellite imagery, drones), are increasingly being used to monitor environmental impacts in real time. These tools can track changes in land use, deforestation, water quality, and pollution levels, providing timely data that allows for more effective mitigation strategies.

II) Mobile Applications for Community Monitoring

Mobile platforms have made it easier for communities to participate in impact monitoring. Mobile applications allow residents to report environmental and social issues, such as illegal logging, water contamination, or labor violations, directly to authorities or project managers. This participatory approach not only enhances monitoring but also ensures that local concerns are addressed promptly.

III) Big Data and Cloud Platforms for Data Aggregation

Cloud platforms and big data analytics are being used to aggregate data from multiple sources, including environmental sensors, social media, and satellite systems. These platforms provide a centralized space for monitoring and evaluating impacts in real-time, enabling stakeholders to make quicker, more informed decisions.

IV) Real-Time Dashboards for Monitoring Key Indicators

Real-time dashboards are increasingly being used to track key environmental, social, and economic indicators. These dashboards present up-to-date information on the performance of a project, enabling decision-makers to assess whether the project is meeting its sustainability targets or requires corrective actions.

V) Challenges in Real-Time Monitoring

While digital tools offer tremendous potential, there are challenges to their widespread use. These include issues related to data privacy, the digital divide, and the need for training and capacity-building. Additionally, real-time monitoring requires a robust infrastructure that may not always be available in remote or underdeveloped regions.

8.6 Conclusion

Emerging trends and innovations in impact assessment are reshaping the way projects are planned, implemented, and evaluated. AI, Big Data, climate change considerations, ESG frameworks, and digital tools are enabling more accurate, inclusive, and real-time assessments. By leveraging these technologies and frameworks, impact assessments can better address the complexities of modern development challenges and help ensure that projects contribute to sustainable, equitable, and resilient futures. However, these innovations also come with challenges that must be carefully managed to ensure that the benefits are fully realized and that no one is left behind in the pursuit of progress.

CHAPTER IX

Ethical Considerations in Impact Assessment

Ethics plays a critical role in the practice of impact assessment (IA), ensuring that the process is conducted with fairness, integrity, and respect for the rights and needs of all stakeholders involved. The primary goal of IA is to evaluate the potential environmental, social, and economic impacts of a project, ensuring that these impacts are understood, minimized, and managed effectively. However, it is not just about the technical accuracy and comprehensiveness of the assessments but also about the ethical considerations that guide the conduct of assessments, decision-making processes, and the management of impacts. These ethical considerations are crucial for the credibility and success of impact assessments and contribute to the creation of projects that are just, equitable, and sustainable.

This chapter explores the ethical dimensions of impact assessment, focusing on the core areas of ethical standards and accountability, transparency and stakeholder participation, human rights and indigenous communities, and ethical dilemmas that can arise during the impact assessment process.

10.1 Ethical Standards and Accountability

Ethical standards are essential to the impact assessment process as they ensure that assessments are conducted with professionalism, integrity, and fairness. These standards not only guide the conduct of environmental and social impact assessments (ESIAs) but also provide a foundation for accountability in decision-making and implementation.

10.1.1 The Importance of Ethical Standards

Ethical standards help impact assessors maintain the highest degree of professionalism and objectivity. They ensure that the data gathered and analyzed during the assessment process is handled honestly and that the potential risks and benefits of the proposed project are evaluated fairly. The inclusion of ethical standards in impact assessments is essential to prevent the manipulation of findings or the suppression of adverse impacts for the benefit of powerful stakeholders.

These standards may include:

I) Objectivity and impartiality: Impact assessors should remain neutral, free from bias, and make decisions based on evidence rather than political or financial considerations.

II) Confidentiality and respect for sensitive information: Sensitive data related to the environment, social groups, or businesses should be protected.

III) Fairness in evaluation: All potential impacts—both positive and negative—should be assessed in a balanced way, taking into account the views of all affected parties.

10.1.2 Accountability in Impact Assessment:

Accountability ensures that those responsible for conducting, reviewing, and approving impact assessments are answerable for their actions. There must be clear mechanisms in place to hold both the assessors and decision-makers accountable for their decisions. This includes ensuring that the impact assessment process is conducted in accordance with legal and regulatory requirements, as well as international ethical norms.

Key aspects of accountability include:

I) Clear documentation: Maintaining accurate and detailed records of the assessment process, methodology, and decision-making ensures transparency and accountability.

II) Independent review: Independent reviews or audits of the impact assessment can help to ensure that the process was conducted ethically and that the findings and recommendations are valid.

III) Responsibility for mitigating impacts: If a project is approved despite adverse impacts, the project proponents are ethically responsible for implementing effective mitigation measures.

IV) Transparency and Stakeholder Participation:One of the fundamental ethical principles in impact assessment is transparency—the openness and accessibility of information to all stakeholders involved in or affected by the project. This principle ensures that stakeholders are informed and have the opportunity to provide input into the assessment process. Stakeholder participation is crucial in achieving this transparency, as it allows affected communities, especially vulnerable groups, to express their concerns and preferences regarding the project.

V) Transparency in the Impact Assessment Process:Transparency involves making information related to the potential impacts of a project, the methodology of the assessment, and the decision-making process available to the public. This can be done by:

Disclosing all relevant information: Project proponents and impact assessors should share the full scope of the proposed project and its potential impacts.

Accessible communication: Information should be communicated in a way that is understandable and accessible to all stakeholders, especially those who might not have technical expertise.

Dissemination of findings: The results of the impact assessments, including both positive and negative impacts, should be publicly disclosed to ensure that the decision-making process is fully transparent.

10.1.3 Stakeholder Participation and Consultation: Stakeholder participation is the process by which individuals or groups who are affected by or have an interest in the proposed project are actively involved in the impact assessment. This process allows for a more comprehensive understanding of the local context, concerns, and needs.

Key principles for effective stakeholder participation include:

Inclusive participation: All relevant stakeholders, particularly vulnerable and marginalized groups, should be included in the process. This may include local communities, indigenous groups, women, youth, and workers.

Early engagement: Stakeholders should be involved early in the planning process, rather than just during the public consultation phase, to ensure that their concerns are addressed from the outset.

Continuous dialogue: Stakeholder engagement should be an ongoing process that allows for feedback and adaptation throughout the life of the project.

By ensuring transparency and meaningful participation, the impact assessment process becomes more democratic and just, ultimately leading to better decisions that reflect the interests and concerns of all stakeholders.

10.3 Human Rights and Indigenous Communities

The recognition and protection of human rights—including the rights of indigenous communities—are critical components of ethical impact assessments. Development projects often affect the most vulnerable groups in society, and it is essential to ensure that these groups' rights are respected, protected, and promoted.

I) Human Rights in Impact Assessment: Human rights are a fundamental consideration in the impact assessment process. The assessment must evaluate how a project could affect the rights of individuals and communities, particularly in terms of:

Access to land and resources: Projects that involve land acquisition or changes in land use must respect the rights of local communities and ensure that they are compensated fairly for any land taken or disrupted.

Right to health and safety: Assessments should address potential risks to public health and ensure that projects are designed to minimize harm to human health.

Right to participation: All individuals should have the right to participate in decisions that affect them, and this must be reflected in the assessment and decision-making process.

Human rights assessments should be incorporated into impact assessments to ensure that the rights of individuals are safeguarded, particularly in the context of land and resource use.

II) Indigenous Rights and Cultural Integrity: Indigenous communities are often disproportionately affected by development projects, especially those that involve land acquisition, natural resource extraction, or infrastructure development. Ethical impact assessments must consider the cultural integrity of indigenous groups and ensure that their free, prior, and informed consent (FPIC) is obtained before any project is implemented.

This principle is enshrined in international law, particularly in instruments such as the United Nations Declaration on the Rights of Indigenous Peoples (UNDRIP), which emphasizes the right of indigenous peoples to maintain their cultural practices, land use, and governance systems.

Incorporating indigenous rights into impact assessments involves:

Consultation and consent: Ensuring that indigenous peoples are consulted before a project begins and that their consent is obtained where required.

Cultural preservation: Protecting the cultural practices, sacred sites, and ways of life of indigenous communities.

Equitable participation: Ensuring that indigenous communities have a fair and meaningful role in the decision-making process.

10.4 Ethical Dilemmas in Impact Assessment

Ethical dilemmas are a natural part of the impact assessment process, as assessors must often navigate complex situations where the interests of various stakeholders conflict, and the trade-offs between development, environmental conservation, and social equity are unclear.

I) Conflicting Interests: In many cases, the interests of different stakeholders may be in direct conflict. For example, a proposed infrastructure project may promise economic development and job creation, but it may also lead to environmental degradation and displacement of vulnerable communities. Assessors face the ethical dilemma of balancing these competing interests and making decisions that may have significant negative consequences for some stakeholders.

II) Trade-offs Between Development and Sustainability: Another ethical challenge involves making decisions about the trade-offs between development and sustainability. In some cases, the economic benefits of a project may be clear, but the environmental or social costs could be high. Assessors must weigh these trade-offs and make recommendations that reflect the principles of sustainable development.

III) Managing Uncertainty and Risk: Ethical dilemmas also arise in situations where there is significant uncertainty or lack of data. For example, when assessing the potential environmental impacts of a project, assessors may not have sufficient information to predict the exact outcomes. In such cases, they must decide how much weight to give to uncertain risks and how to prioritize precautionary measures without unnecessarily hindering development.

10.5 Conclusion

Ethical considerations are integral to the success and credibility of impact assessments. Adherence to ethical standards ensures that the process is conducted fairly, transparently, and with respect for the rights and needs of all stakeholders. By incorporating principles of human rights, transparency, stakeholder participation, and accountability into impact assessments, practitioners can ensure that projects are not only viable but also socially responsible and environmentally sustainable. The ethical challenges and dilemmas that arise during impact assessments require careful consideration and balance, but with a commitment to ethical practices, impact assessments can contribute to creating more equitable, just, and sustainable development outcomes.

CHAPTER X

Policy and Legal Frameworks for Impact Assessment

Impact assessments are central to ensuring that projects, particularly those in development, infrastructure, and industry, contribute to sustainable development while minimizing negative effects on the environment, society, and economy. Policies, legal frameworks, and international conventions govern how these assessments are conducted. In this chapter, we will explore the global policies and conventions guiding impact assessment, national legal and policy frameworks from multiple countries, and the role of government and institutions in overseeing and implementing impact assessments. This comprehensive approach ensures that impact assessments are standardized, thorough, and aligned with global development goals.

9.1 Global Policies and Conventions

9.1.1 The United Nations Environmental Policies

The United Nations (UN) has been at the forefront of promoting global standards for environmental sustainability, social development, and economic well-being. Several key environmental policies and frameworks established by the UN play a significant role in shaping how impact assessments are carried out globally.

I. Agenda 21 and the Rio Declaration: A Foundation for Sustainable Development

The United Nations Conference on Environment and Development (UNCED), held in Rio de Janeiro in 1992, is considered a landmark event in the global pursuit of sustainable development. The conference, often referred to as the "Earth Summit," brought together representatives from over 170 countries, along with non-governmental organizations, businesses, and other stakeholders, to discuss and promote global environmental and development issues. The key outcomes of the summit included the Rio Declaration on Environment and Development and Agenda 21, both of which provided a comprehensive framework for promoting sustainable development worldwide.

These two documents have had a profound influence on shaping national and international policies related to environmental protection, social development, and economic growth. They introduced the concept of sustainability as an integrated approach to development, balancing the needs of the present with the ability of future generations to meet their own needs. Furthermore, the frameworks outlined in these documents have significantly shaped how environmental and social impact assessments are conducted, influencing the methods used for evaluating the effects of various projects on people, society, and the planet.

I) The Rio Declaration: Guiding Principles for Sustainable Development

The Rio Declaration on Environment and Development is a set of 27 principles that outline the fundamental rights and responsibilities of nations in the context of environmental protection and sustainable development. These principles emphasize the need for cooperation among governments, businesses, and individuals to achieve environmental sustainability while promoting social and economic development. The Declaration set out key guiding principles, some of which are especially relevant to impact assessments:

a) Principle 1 - Human Rights and the Environment

This principle recognizes that human beings are at the center of sustainable development, and that they are entitled to a healthy and productive life in harmony with nature. It highlights the connection between human well-being and environmental quality, laying the foundation for environmental impact assessments (EIA) to consider human health, livelihood, and community well-being as central to their evaluations.

b) Principle 4 - Sustainable Development

This principle emphasizes the need for the integration of environmental protection and social development. It underlines the importance of achieving economic development without compromising the environment for future generations. This idea of sustainable development has become a central tenet of impact assessments, where projects are required to evaluate both the short-term benefits and the long-term environmental, social, and economic costs.

c) Principle 10 - Public Participation

Principle 10 calls for active public participation in decision-making, particularly for projects with significant environmental and social impacts. The principle stresses the need for access to information, public hearings, and transparent decision-making processes. Public participation has become a core component of modern EIA processes, ensuring that local communities, affected stakeholders, and other interest groups are involved in assessing and mitigating potential impacts.

d) Principle 15 - Precautionary Approach

The precautionary principle advocates for taking preventive action in the face of environmental threats, even when scientific evidence is not conclusive. This principle has become central in many environmental impact assessments, requiring projects to adopt preventive measures if there is uncertainty about the potential risks to the environment or society.

Agenda 21: A Blueprint for Global Sustainable Development

Agenda 21, adopted during the Earth Summit, is an action plan that provides specific recommendations for governments, businesses, and other stakeholders to promote sustainable development at local, national, and global levels. The document is comprehensive, covering a broad range of issues, from poverty reduction to biodiversity conservation, and is divided into 40 chapters.

The document recognizes that sustainable development must involve a holistic approach that includes social, economic, and environmental considerations. The following key elements of Agenda 21 are particularly relevant to impact assessments:

A. Integrating Environmental Considerations into Development Planning

Agenda 21 emphasizes the need to integrate environmental concerns into all development planning processes. This means that environmental assessments must be conducted early in the project planning stages to understand and mitigate potential risks. By promoting the integration of environmental, social, and economic considerations, Agenda 21 encourages policymakers to take a balanced approach to development that considers the needs of both current and future generations.

I) Chapter 4: Changing Consumption Patterns

One of the central themes of Agenda 21 is the need to address unsustainable consumption patterns, particularly in industrialized countries. Impact assessments in various sectors—such as industrial, agricultural, and urban development—are increasingly required to consider the impacts of consumption on natural resources, ecosystems, and local communities. This focus on sustainable consumption has contributed to the widespread adoption of practices like lifecycle assessments and resource efficiency audits in project evaluations.

II) Chapter 7: Promoting Sustainable Human Settlements Development

Urbanization and the rapid expansion of human settlements pose significant challenges to environmental sustainability. Chapter 7 of Agenda 21 promotes the development of sustainable cities and towns, advocating for the integration of environmental and social considerations into urban planning. Environmental and social impact assessments (ESIA) for urban development projects must now address issues such as access to clean water, waste management, transportation, and the impact on local ecosystems, all of which are central to the principles outlined in Agenda 21.

III) Chapter 8: Integrating the Environment and Development in Decision-Making

This chapter calls for environmental considerations to be systematically integrated into the decision-making processes at all levels of government, business, and civil society. As a result, impact assessments have become a key tool for decision-makers, enabling them to evaluate potential trade-offs between development objectives and environmental/social impacts. It has been a catalyst for integrating sustainability into policy frameworks, ensuring that development decisions do not undermine environmental integrity or social well-being.

IV) Chapter 36: Promoting Education, Public Awareness, and Training

Agenda 21 recognizes the importance of education and public awareness in promoting sustainable development. It advocates for the inclusion of sustainability principles in school curricula, public outreach, and community engagement initiatives. As a result, impact assessments have increasingly focused on public consultation and the dissemination of information to stakeholders. The success of many projects now depends on how well communities understand the potential impacts and the steps being taken to mitigate them.

9.2 Influence of Agenda 21 and the Rio Declaration on Impact Assessments

Since their adoption, the principles outlined in the Rio Declaration and Agenda 21 have had a profound impact on how environmental and social assessments are conducted. These documents helped to formalize the concept of sustainable development and provided clear guidelines on how to evaluate and address the broader impacts of development projects.

9.2.1 Comprehensive Impact Assessments

The principles in Agenda 21 and the Rio Declaration have pushed for more comprehensive approaches to impact assessment. Traditional environmental impact assessments have expanded to include social and economic dimensions, ensuring that the holistic impacts of projects are evaluated. The integration of sustainability into project assessments, as outlined in Agenda 21, has become the standard in many countries, helping to shape policies and practices in environmental protection, social equity, and economic development.

9.2.2 Public Participation and Transparency

The emphasis on public participation, particularly through Principle 10 of the Rio Declaration, has led to the development of robust mechanisms for community engagement in impact assessments. In many countries, laws now require public hearings, consultation processes, and access to information for projects that may have significant environmental or social impacts. These participatory mechanisms ensure that the voices of affected communities and stakeholders are heard and considered, which ultimately leads to more informed and balanced decisions.

9.2.3 Precautionary Principle and Risk Management

Principle 15 of the Rio Declaration, which calls for a precautionary approach in the face of environmental uncertainty, has influenced how impact assessments handle risk. In cases where potential risks are uncertain but could have serious consequences, project developers are encouraged to adopt the "precautionary principle," taking preventive measures to avoid or minimize harm. This has been integrated into modern EIA practices, with an emphasis on mitigating uncertainty and adopting strategies that prioritize environmental protection over economic gain.

9.3 Sustainable Development Goals (SDGs)

The adoption of the SDGs in 2015 built upon the framework established by Agenda 21, further reinforcing the need for environmental and social considerations in development planning. The SDGs have become the guiding reference for governments, businesses, and organizations seeking to promote sustainable development through their projects. As a result, impact assessments now increasingly align with SDG targets, especially those related to poverty eradication, sustainable cities, climate action, and reduced inequalities.

Agenda 21 and the Rio Declaration, adopted at the Earth Summit in 1992, were revolutionary documents that shaped the global approach to sustainable development. They provided a detailed framework for integrating environmental, social, and economic concerns into development planning and decision-making. These documents laid the foundation for the modern practices of environmental and social impact assessments, guiding the process by which governments, businesses, and organizations assess the potential risks and benefits of development projects. As the world continues to grapple with global challenges such as climate change, resource depletion, and social inequality, the principles outlined in Agenda 21 and the Rio Declaration remain as relevant as ever in guiding sustainable development. Adopted by all UN member states in 2015, the SDGs are a universal call to action to end poverty, protect the planet, and ensure prosperity for all. The SDGs cover a broad range of goals, including climate action (SDG 13), responsible consumption and production (SDG 12), and sustainable cities and communities (SDG 11). Impact assessments are now increasingly aligned with these goals, which guide both the evaluation and development of policies, projects, and programs at the global and local levels.

9.4 Environmental Impact Assessment (EIA) Procedures

The UN Environment Programme (UNEP) has been instrumental in providing guidelines for conducting Environmental Impact Assessments (EIA). The UNEP's "Environmental Impact Assessment: A Guide to Best Practice" offers global standards for EIAs and highlights the importance of considering biodiversity, ecosystem services, and community welfare in decision-making.

9.4.1 Convention on Biological Diversity (CBD)

The CBD, adopted in 1992, is a key international agreement that requires parties to integrate biodiversity conservation into development projects and activities. The CBD emphasizes the need for conducting environmental impact assessments in projects that may affect biodiversity, with an emphasis on public participation and the consideration of alternative solutions.

9.4.2 The Paris Agreement on Climate Change

The Paris Agreement, adopted in 2015, focuses on limiting global warming to well below 2 degrees Celsius compared to pre-industrial levels. This agreement sets out the requirement for countries to integrate climate change considerations into their development projects, including impact assessments. It mandates that projects must consider their carbon footprints and long-term climate resilience in their environmental assessments.

9.4.3 World Bank and ADB Guidelines

I) World Bank Environmental and Social Framework (ESF)

The World Bank's ESF, adopted in 2016, provides a comprehensive framework for addressing environmental and social risks in the projects it finances. The framework consists of ten environmental and social standards, which guide impact assessments for the projects. These standards focus on issues such as labor and working conditions, health and safety, biodiversity conservation, and community engagement. The ESF underscores the importance of environmental and social management plans (ESMPs) that are built into project design from the outset.

II) Environmental and Social Risk Management: The World Bank emphasizes the integration of environmental and social risk management practices in projects, ensuring that the negative impacts of development are minimized.

III) Stakeholder Engagement and Grievance Redress: A crucial aspect of the World Bank's guidelines is ensuring that project stakeholders are actively engaged throughout the impact assessment process. This engagement must be transparent, inclusive, and meaningful, with adequate mechanisms for addressing grievances.

IV) Asian Development Bank (ADB) Safeguard Policy: The ADB's Safeguard Policy, which was updated in 2009 and further refined in 2019, requires that its funded projects undergo a thorough impact assessment, including the consideration of environmental, social, and gender risks. The Safeguard Policy addresses the need for:

Environmental Protection: Ensuring that projects comply with international environmental standards and local regulations.

Social Safeguards: Including the resettlement and livelihoods of affected communities, especially vulnerable groups such as indigenous people and women.

Climate Change Considerations: Aligning project activities with efforts to mitigate and adapt to climate change.

The ADB also emphasizes the importance of participatory approaches in assessing and managing the environmental and social impacts of projects, fostering collaboration among stakeholders to identify risks and mitigation strategies.

9.5 National Legal and Policy Frameworks (with Examples from Multiple Countries)

National governments are responsible for the enactment and enforcement of policies and laws that regulate impact assessments within their respective territories. Each country develops its own set of laws and frameworks that are designed to ensure that development projects proceed with minimal adverse impacts on the environment and society.

9.5 1. United States: National Environmental Policy Act (NEPA)

The National Environmental Policy Act (NEPA) was enacted in 1970 in the United States and is one of the most influential pieces of environmental legislation. NEPA requires federal agencies to assess the environmental effects of their proposed actions before making decisions. This includes an assessment of potential impacts on air, water, wildlife, and human health. The key aspects of NEPA include:

Environmental Impact Statements (EIS): Comprehensive reports that analyze the environmental effects of proposed federal actions, including alternatives and mitigation strategies.

Public Participation: A core feature of NEPA is public participation, which allows communities, environmental organizations, and other stakeholders to provide input on proposed projects.

9.5.2 . India: The Environment Protection Act and EIA Notification

India's legal framework for environmental impact assessments is primarily governed by the Environment Protection Act, 1986, and the EIA Notification of 2006, which was amended several times. The EIA process in India requires the assessment of potential environmental impacts for specific categories of projects, including industrial development, mining, infrastructure, and urbanization. Key features of India's framework include:

Categorization of Projects: The EIA Notification categorizes projects based on their scale, location, and potential environmental impact. Projects falling under certain categories must undergo mandatory EIA.

Public Consultation: Public consultation is an integral part of India's EIA process, allowing local communities and stakeholders to voice their concerns regarding proposed projects.

State-Level Monitoring: Each state in India is responsible for ensuring that projects comply with national environmental regulations.

9.5.3. European Union: Strategic Environmental Assessment (SEA) and EIA Directives

The European Union has a comprehensive framework for environmental impact assessments, which includes both the EIA and the Strategic Environmental Assessment (SEA) Directives. The EIA Directive mandates that projects likely to have significant environmental effects must be subject to an impact assessment before development. The SEA Directive, which applies to plans and programs, ensures that environmental considerations are integrated into the planning process. Both directives emphasize:

Public Participation: Ensuring that the public is consulted during the planning stages of projects.

Alternatives and Mitigation: Projects must assess alternative approaches and propose mitigation measures for any identified adverse impacts.

9.6 Role of Government and Institutions in Impact Assessment

Governments and institutions play a crucial role in the successful implementation of impact assessments. Their responsibilities include setting the legal framework, ensuring compliance, and overseeing the process from project inception to completion.

9.6.1. Role of Government in Regulating Impact Assessment

Governments are primarily responsible for creating and enforcing laws and regulations that mandate impact assessments. They set the legal standards for how assessments should be conducted, ensure that projects meet these standards, and ensure that affected communities are consulted. Key functions of government in impact assessment include:

Legislation and Policy Development: Governments establish the legal foundation for conducting environmental, social, and economic impact assessments, including establishing specific regulations and standards for different sectors.

Enforcement and Monitoring: Governments ensure that impact assessments are conducted in compliance with legal requirements, monitoring projects during implementation to ensure that mitigation measures are effectively carried out.

Public Participation: Governments facilitate public consultation and the involvement of affected communities and stakeholders in the assessment process.

9.6.2. Role of Environmental and Social Agencies

Several national and international agencies are responsible for overseeing the conduct of impact assessments, monitoring project implementation, and ensuring that sustainable practices are followed:

Environmental Protection Agencies: These agencies are tasked with regulating and monitoring the environmental impacts of projects, ensuring compliance with environmental laws, and enforcing penalties for violations.

Social and Labor Agencies: These institutions focus on the social impacts of projects, including issues related to human rights, resettlement, and labor conditions.

Local Government and Planning Authorities: Local authorities often play a role in implementing impact assessments, ensuring that regional or community concerns are adequately addressed.

9.7 Conclusion

The policy and legal frameworks for impact assessments are essential for ensuring that development projects proceed responsibly, minimizing harm to the environment, society, and economy. At the global level, international conventions and guidelines provide a foundation for sustainable development. At the national level, governments develop specific policies and laws tailored to their local contexts. The role of governments and institutions is pivotal in ensuring that impact assessments are effectively conducted, monitored, and enforced. The evolving nature of global challenges, such as climate change and biodiversity loss, will continue to shape the development of impact assessment policies, making it imperative for countries to strengthen their frameworks and align them with global sustainability goals.

CHAPTER XI

Future of Impact Assessment

As development projects evolve and the world faces unprecedented environmental and social challenges, impact assessments (IAs) are becoming increasingly critical in guiding sustainable development. The future of impact assessment lies in its capacity to adapt to changing circumstances, integrate new technologies, foster global collaboration, and drive solutions that contribute to a more sustainable and equitable future. This chapter explores key aspects of the future of impact assessments, including adaptive management, technology-driven impact assessments, strengthening global cooperation, and the pursuit of sustainability.

11.1 Adaptive Management in Impact Assessment

Adaptive management is a flexible, systematic approach to managing projects and policies in the face of uncertainty. It is particularly relevant in the context of impact assessment, as it allows for continuous learning and improvement over time. This approach is grounded in the recognition that development projects often involve complex systems that are difficult to predict and control, and that conditions can **change during the course of a project.**

11.1.1 Principles of Adaptive Management

Adaptive management involves a continuous cycle of planning, implementation, monitoring, evaluation, and adjustment. The main goal is to ensure that projects can be adjusted as new information or unexpected conditions arise. This is especially important for projects with long-term impacts, such as infrastructure developments or natural resource management projects.

I) Monitoring and Feedback: Regular monitoring of environmental, social, and economic impacts allows for timely identification of issues and the adjustment of strategies to mitigate or enhance these impacts.

II) Learning from Experience: Adaptive management encourages learning from past decisions and outcomes, ensuring that future decisions are based on experience and evidence rather than assumptions.

III) Flexibility in Implementation: When conditions change, adaptive management allows for flexibility in the design and implementation of mitigation measures or project modifications.

11.1.2 Adaptive Management in Impact Assessments

In the context of impact assessment, adaptive management involves incorporating flexibility into the assessment process. For example, it can involve:

Updating environmental or social impact models based on new data as a project progresses.

Adjusting mitigation strategies if monitoring reveals unforeseen impacts.

Engaging stakeholders throughout the project lifecycle to ensure that the assessment remains relevant to changing conditions.

Adaptive management helps to reduce uncertainty and allows for more resilient, responsive, and sustainable project outcomes. It also ensures that impact assessments remain relevant and effective over time, even as circumstances evolve.

11.2 Technology-Driven Impact Assessments

Advancements in technology are transforming how impact assessments are conducted. Technology is enabling more accurate, efficient, and comprehensive assessments by providing tools to analyze data, model impacts, and engage stakeholders. As we look to the future of impact assessments, technology will continue to play an increasingly central role in enhancing the effectiveness of assessments and supporting sustainable decision-making.

11.2.1 Key Technologies in Impact Assessment

I) Geospatial Technologies (GIS and Remote Sensing): Geographic Information Systems (GIS) and remote sensing technologies allow for detailed mapping of environmental features, land use patterns, and other spatial data. These tools enable assessors to analyze the potential impacts of a project on ecosystems, water resources, and urban environments with greater accuracy. GIS is also used to track and monitor changes in the environment over time, helping to improve adaptive management practices.

II) Big Data and Artificial Intelligence (AI): Big data analytics allows for the processing and analysis of vast amounts of data from various sources. AI can be used to identify patterns, predict outcomes, and recommend appropriate mitigation measures. For example, AI-powered models can predict the potential environmental impacts of a project or forecast the economic effects of a new development. By analyzing historical data and real-time information, AI can provide deeper insights and more reliable predictions.

III) Environmental Simulation and Modeling: Simulation tools and environmental models can replicate real-world conditions to assess the potential impacts of a project. For example, environmental models can simulate air and water quality changes due to industrial emissions or deforestation. These models help assessors understand complex interactions between various environmental and social systems and predict the long-term consequences of a project.

IV) Blockchain for Transparency and Accountability: Blockchain technology can be used to create transparent, immutable records of impact assessments, stakeholder consultations, and mitigation measures. By ensuring that data is securely stored and publicly accessible, blockchain can enhance trust in the impact assessment process and prevent manipulation or misreporting.

V) Virtual Reality (VR) and Augmented Reality (AR): VR and AR are emerging tools that can enhance stakeholder engagement in impact assessments. These technologies allow stakeholders to experience and visualize potential changes in their environment before a project is implemented. For example, VR can simulate the impact of a new road or building on the local landscape, helping communities and decision-makers understand the potential consequences of a development.

11.2.2 Benefits of Technology-Driven Impact Assessments

The integration of technology in impact assessments offers several benefits:

I) Increased accuracy and efficiency: Technologies like GIS, AI, and big data analytics allow for faster, more accurate data collection and analysis.

II) Enhanced stakeholder engagement: Interactive technologies such as VR and AR can improve communication with stakeholders and increase their involvement in decision-making processes.

III) Better predictive capabilities: AI and environmental models can predict the potential long-term impacts of a project, allowing for more informed decisions.

IV) Improved monitoring: Remote sensing and IoT-based monitoring systems provide real-time data on environmental and social conditions, making it easier to track impacts and implement adaptive management strategies.

11.3 Strengthening Global Cooperation for Impact Assessments

As global challenges such as climate change, biodiversity loss, and social inequality continue to intensify, there is a growing need for global cooperation in the field of impact assessment. Environmental and social impacts do not adhere to national borders, and international collaboration is crucial to ensure that projects are assessed comprehensively and responsibly.

11.3.1 Global Standards and Frameworks

One of the key areas for strengthening global cooperation is the development and adoption of global standards for impact assessments. Various international organizations, including the United Nations (UN), the World Bank, and the Asian Development Bank (ADB), have established guidelines for environmental and social assessments. However, the implementation of these standards often varies across regions, leading to discrepancies in the quality and rigor of impact assessments.

Efforts to standardize the impact assessment process include:

I) Harmonizing methodologies: Creating standardized tools and methodologies for conducting impact assessments can facilitate cross-border cooperation and ensure that assessments are consistent and comparable across countries.

II) International collaboration: Strengthening cooperation between governments, international organizations, and private sector entities can lead to the sharing of best practices and resources, improving the quality of impact assessments worldwide.

11.3.2 Capacity Building for Impact Assessment

Building capacity in developing countries is crucial to ensuring that impact assessments are conducted effectively and in accordance with international standards. This involves:

I) Training assessors and regulators: Ensuring that impact assessors are trained in the latest methodologies and technologies is essential to improving the quality of impact assessments.

II) Developing local expertise: Promoting local expertise in environmental and social impact assessments helps to build trust with stakeholders and ensures that assessments are sensitive to local conditions and needs.

11.4 Cross-Border Environmental and Social Considerations

Global cooperation is also necessary for addressing transboundary environmental and social impacts. For example, a large infrastructure project in one country may have environmental consequences for neighboring countries, such as pollution, deforestation, or changes in water resources. Cooperation between governments and stakeholders across borders is essential to manage these impacts effectively.

International treaties and agreements, such as the Convention on Biological Diversity (CBD) and the Paris Agreement on climate change, also play a crucial role in guiding impact assessments for projects with global implications.

11.5 Toward a Sustainable Future

The ultimate goal of impact assessments is to guide development toward a sustainable future—one where economic growth, social equity, and environmental protection are balanced. As the world faces growing challenges such as climate change, resource depletion, and social inequality, impact assessments will continue to play a critical role in shaping projects that support sustainable development.

11.5.1 Promoting Sustainability through Impact Assessments

Impact assessments contribute to sustainability by:

I) Identifying long-term impacts: Assessments help decision-makers understand the long-term consequences of a project, including environmental degradation, social disruption, and economic inequality.

II) Recommending mitigation strategies: By identifying potential adverse impacts, impact assessments provide recommendations for mitigating these impacts, ensuring that projects are designed to be as sustainable as possible.

III) Encouraging sustainable practices: The assessment process encourages the adoption of sustainable practices, such as the use of renewable resources, the reduction of waste, and the protection of ecosystems.

11.6 Sustainable Development Goals (SDGs)

The United Nations Sustainable Development Goals (SDGs) provide a global framework for achieving sustainability by 2030. Impact assessments play a crucial role in ensuring that projects align with the SDGs and contribute to achieving these global objectives. For example, assessments can help ensure that projects promote clean water and sanitation (SDG 6), affordable and clean energy (SDG 7), and reduced inequalities (SDG 10).

11.7 The Future of Sustainable Development

As the future of impact assessments evolves, the focus will increasingly shift toward projects that foster sustainability in all its dimensions. This includes ensuring that development projects:

Contribute to the well-being of future generations by minimizing environmental degradation.

Promote social equity by considering the needs of marginalized groups and fostering inclusive economic growth.

Use innovative technologies and solutions that enable more sustainable and efficient practices.

By embracing adaptive management, leveraging technology, fostering global cooperation, and prioritizing sustainability, the future of impact assessments can contribute to a more resilient, equitable, and sustainable world.

11.8 Conclusion

The future of impact assessments is one of innovation, adaptation, and collaboration. As the world faces complex challenges, impact assessments will continue to evolve, integrating new technologies, adopting more flexible and responsive approaches, and fostering greater global cooperation. By focusing on sustainability and the long-term well-being of communities and ecosystems, impact assessments can play a pivotal role in guiding development toward a more sustainable future.

Guide For Impact Assessment

<u>**I. A Guide for the Process of Participatory Rural Appraisal (PRA)**</u>

Participatory Rural Appraisal (PRA) is a widely adopted approach to engage communities in the development process, enabling them to identify, analyze, and act upon their priorities and problems. The PRA methodology emphasizes local knowledge and promotes active participation of community members. Below is a detailed exploration of the PRA process, encompassing its stages, tools, techniques, and applications.

1. Preparation Stage

Objective: Create a conducive environment for PRA by building rapport with the community and preparing logistics for effective engagement.

Steps:

1. Defining Objectives:

o Clearly articulate the purpose of conducting PRA, such as needs assessment, project planning, or resource mapping.

o Align objectives with the specific goals of stakeholders and development partners.

2. Team Formation:

o Assemble a multidisciplinary team with skills in facilitation, observation, and communication.

o Train team members in PRA principles and tools to ensure consistency in methodology.

3. Selection of Community:

o Identify the community based on the objectives and context of the PRA.

o Consider criteria such as geographic diversity, socioeconomic characteristics, and development needs.

4. Building Rapport:

o Establish trust with the community through initial visits and informal interactions.

o Communicate the purpose and benefits of PRA to gain acceptance and participation.

5. Logistics and Planning:

o Schedule activities at times convenient for the community.

o Arrange for materials, transportation, and accommodation if required.

2. Data Collection and Engagement

Objective: Gather qualitative and quantitative data through participatory methods while fostering community involvement.

Steps:

1. Community Mapping:

o Use tools such as social mapping and resource mapping to understand the spatial and social dynamics of the community.

o Encourage community members to create maps using simple materials like chalk, sand, or paper.

2. Seasonal Calendars:

o Develop seasonal calendars to capture information about agricultural activities, income sources, health issues, and migration patterns.

o Discuss patterns and variations over time to understand challenges and opportunities.

3. Transect Walks:

o Conduct systematic walks through the community to observe resources, infrastructure, and environmental conditions.

o Engage community members to explain observations and provide context.

4. Focus Group Discussions (FGDs):

o Organize group discussions with specific demographics such as women, youth, or elders.

o Use semi-structured questions to explore issues, priorities, and potential solutions.

5. Ranking and Scoring:

o Facilitate pairwise ranking and matrix scoring exercises to prioritize issues, resources, or interventions.

o Encourage diverse participation to capture varying perspectives.

6. Timelines and Historical Analysis:

o Document key events and changes in the community over time to understand historical trends.

o Use tools like timelines or historical profiles created by community members.

7. Problem Tree Analysis:

o Identify core problems and their root causes through a visual representation.

o Discuss the interrelationships between issues to guide problem-solving efforts.

3. Data Synthesis and Analysis

Objective: Organize and interpret collected data to derive actionable insights and prioritize interventions.

Steps:

1. Data Compilation:

o Consolidate information from maps, charts, and discussions into a comprehensive database.

o Document qualitative insights alongside quantitative metrics.

2. Validation with Community:

o Present findings to the community for feedback and verification.

o Encourage open discussions to refine and confirm interpretations.

3. Thematic Analysis:

o Identify recurring themes and patterns in the data.

o Classify findings under categories such as resources, challenges, opportunities, and needs.

4. Prioritization:

o Collaboratively rank identified issues based on their significance and feasibility of intervention.

o Ensure representation from different community groups in the prioritization process.

5. Action Planning:

o Develop an action plan with clear objectives, timelines, and responsibilities.

o Outline resource requirements and potential support mechanisms.

4. Implementation and Follow-Up

Objective: Translate findings into actionable interventions and ensure sustained community involvement.

Steps:

1. Capacity Building:

o Train community members in skills required for implementing identified projects.

o Strengthen local institutions to manage and sustain development initiatives.

2. Resource Mobilization:

o Identify and secure resources from internal and external sources.

o Leverage community contributions to enhance ownership and accountability.

3. Implementation of Activities:

o Execute planned interventions in collaboration with the community.

o Ensure transparency and inclusivity in decision-making and resource allocation.

4. Monitoring and Evaluation (M&E):

o Establish M&E frameworks to track progress and outcomes.

o Use participatory methods like community scorecards or feedback sessions.

5. Feedback Loops:

o Maintain open channels for community feedback throughout implementation.

o Adapt plans based on emerging needs and challenges.

6. Sustainability Planning:

o Develop strategies for long-term maintenance and scaling of successful initiatives.

o Foster partnerships with local governments and organizations to ensure continuity.

5. Tools and Techniques in PRA

1. Participatory Mapping:

o Tools: Social maps, resource maps, transect maps.

o Purpose: Visualize spatial relationships and resource distribution.

2. Time-Related Tools:

o Tools: Seasonal calendars, timelines, trend analysis.

o Purpose: Capture temporal variations and historical changes.

3. Ranking and Scoring:

o Tools: Pairwise ranking, matrix scoring.

o Purpose: Prioritize issues or options based on community preferences.

4. Visual Aids:

o Tools: Charts, diagrams, Venn diagrams.

o Purpose: Facilitate discussions and ensure inclusivity.

5. Interview and Discussion Tools:

o Tools: Semi-structured interviews, focus group discussions.

o Purpose: Gather in-depth qualitative insights.

6. Observation:

o Tools: Transect walks, direct observation.

o Purpose: Understand community dynamics and contextual factors.

6. Principles of PRA

1. Participation:

o Emphasize active involvement of all community members, particularly marginalized groups.

2. Flexibility:

o Adapt methods and tools to suit the context and needs of the community.

3. Respect for Local Knowledge:

o Value indigenous knowledge and incorporate it into analysis and planning.

4. Facilitation, Not Domination:

o Act as facilitators to guide discussions and empower community decision-making.

5. Sustainability:

o Focus on long-term impacts and community ownership of initiatives.

7. Challenges in PRA

1. Power Dynamics:

o Address inequalities that may hinder genuine participation.

2. Cultural Sensitivities:

o Be mindful of cultural norms and values to build trust and avoid conflict.

3. Resource Constraints:

o Ensure adequate resources and time to conduct PRA effectively.

4. Capacity Gaps:

o Invest in training facilitators and community members to enhance their capabilities.

5. Sustaining Engagement:

o Maintain momentum and interest among community members over time.

8. Case Studies and Applications

1. Natural Resource Management:

o Example: Using resource mapping to plan watershed management initiatives.

2. Health and Sanitation:

o Example: Engaging communities to identify health challenges and design interventions.

3. Agriculture and Livelihoods:

o Example: Developing seasonal calendars to optimize agricultural planning.

4. Disaster Risk Reduction:

o Example: Mapping vulnerabilities to enhance disaster preparedness.

5. Education:

o Example: Identifying barriers to education through focus group discussions with parents and teachers.

Participatory Rural Appraisal is a transformative approach that empowers communities to take charge of their development. By fostering collaboration, leveraging local knowledge, and ensuring inclusivity, PRA can lead to sustainable and impactful outcomes. While challenges exist, careful planning, facilitation, and follow-up can maximize its effectiveness, making it a cornerstone of community-driven development efforts.

II. A Guide for the process of Logical Framework Approach (LFA):

The Logical Framework Approach (LFA) is a systematic planning tool widely used in project management, especially in development and humanitarian projects. It ensures that projects are well-structured, results-oriented, and aligned with stakeholder needs. This guide will elaborate on the LFA process, its stages, and how it helps achieve project success.

Introduction to LFA

The Logical Framework Approach originated in the 1960s as a response to the growing need for a structured methodology to design and evaluate projects. It offers a clear structure to:

1. Define project objectives.

2. Identify key assumptions and risks.

3. Monitor and evaluate project progress.

The core output of LFA is the Logical Framework Matrix (Logframe), which provides a concise summary of the project's objectives, indicators, means of verification, and assumptions.

Stages of LFA

The LFA process consists of two main phases:

1. Analysis Phase

2. Planning Phase

Each phase is broken down into specific steps to ensure thoroughness and clarity.

1. Analysis Phase

The Analysis Phase is the foundation of the LFA. It focuses on understanding the context, identifying stakeholders, and diagnosing problems.

Step 1: Stakeholder Analysis

The first step is to identify all stakeholders who might affect or be affected by the project. This includes individuals, groups, and institutions. Key activities in this step include:

• Identifying stakeholders: List all potential stakeholders, such as beneficiaries, funders, local authorities, and NGOs.

• Analyzing interests: Understand each stakeholder's needs, concerns, and potential contributions.

• Assessing influence and importance: Determine the power and impact of each stakeholder on the project.

The output is a stakeholder matrix that categorizes stakeholders based on their influence and interest.

Step 2: Problem Analysis

The second step is to identify the core problem the project aims to address. This involves:

• Identifying problems: Engage stakeholders in brainstorming sessions to identify issues.

• Structuring problems: Use a problem tree to map out the main problem, its causes, and its effects.

The problem tree visualizes the relationships between root causes, the core problem, and its consequences, providing a clear basis for defining project objectives.

Step 3: Objective Analysis

The objective analysis transforms the problem tree into a positive framework, known as the objective tree. This involves:

• Rephrasing problems as objectives: For example, "High unemployment" becomes "Increased employment opportunities."

• Establishing cause-effect relationships: Ensure objectives logically lead to the desired impact.

The objective tree serves as a blueprint for the project's desired outcomes.

Step 4: Strategy Analysis

This step focuses on determining the best approach to achieve the objectives. It includes:

• Identifying alternatives: Explore various strategies to address the core problem.

• Assessing feasibility: Evaluate the cost, benefits, risks, and stakeholder alignment of each option.

• Selecting a strategy: Choose the most effective and feasible approach.

The chosen strategy will form the basis of the project plan.

2. Planning Phase

The Planning Phase builds on the insights gained during the Analysis Phase to develop a comprehensive project plan. The key output of this phase is the Logical Framework Matrix.

Step 1: Developing the Logical Framework Matrix

The Logframe is a structured summary of the project plan. It consists of four main rows:

1. Goal: The overarching aim of the project.

2. Outcomes: Specific changes or benefits the project seeks to achieve.

3. Outputs: Tangible products or services delivered by the project.

4. Activities: Tasks and actions required to deliver the outputs.

Each row is broken down into four columns:

• Narrative Summary: Describes the objective.

• Objectively Verifiable Indicators (OVIs): Metrics to measure success.

• Means of Verification (MoVs): Data sources and methods to track indicators.

• Assumptions: External factors that may influence success.

Step 2: Defining Indicators and Means of Verification

Indicators are critical for monitoring and evaluating progress. They should be:

• Specific: Clearly defined and unambiguous.

• Measurable: Quantifiable to track progress.

• Achievable: Realistic given the project's resources.

• Relevant: Directly linked to the objective.

• Time-bound: Set within a specific timeframe.

Means of Verification (MoVs) outline how data for these indicators will be collected, such as surveys, reports, or field visits.

Step 3: Risk Management

Assumptions identified in the Logframe highlight potential risks. Effective risk management involves:

• Identifying risks: Assess what could go wrong.

• Analyzing impact and likelihood: Determine the significance of each risk.

• Developing mitigation strategies: Outline actions to minimize or manage risks.

A risk matrix can be used to prioritize risks based on their likelihood and impact.

Step 4: Resource Planning

Resource planning ensures the project has the necessary inputs to succeed. This includes:

• Human resources: Define roles, responsibilities, and skills needed.

• Financial resources: Develop a detailed budget.

• Material resources: List equipment, tools, and supplies required.

Step 5: Developing a Work Plan

A work plan outlines the timeline and sequence of activities. Key components include:

• Gantt Chart: A visual representation of the schedule.

• Milestones: Key points of progress.

• Dependencies: Relationships between tasks.

Implementation and Monitoring

Once the planning phase is complete, the project moves into implementation. The LFA continues to guide activities through:

• Regular Monitoring: Track progress against indicators.

• Adjustments: Update the Logframe and plans as needed.

• Stakeholder Engagement: Maintain communication and collaboration.

Evaluation and Lessons Learned

At the end of the project, the LFA supports evaluation by:

• Comparing results to objectives.

• Assessing the effectiveness and efficiency of the project.

• Documenting lessons learned for future initiatives.

The Logical Framework Approach is a robust tool for project design, management, and evaluation. By following its structured process, organizations can ensure their projects are aligned with stakeholder needs, focused on results, and adaptive to challenges. The LFA not only enhances the likelihood of success but also provides a transparent framework for accountability and learning.

III. Guide for Methods of Community Participation

Community participation is a cornerstone of sustainable development, fostering inclusive decision-making and empowering individuals and groups. Various methods are used to ensure that community members are meaningfully engaged in planning, implementing, and evaluating projects. This article explores the different methods of community participation, categorizing them into direct and indirect approaches, formal and informal mechanisms, and context-specific strategies.

1. Informative Participation

Informative participation is the foundational level of community involvement, focusing on ensuring that community members are aware of the issues, projects, and decisions that might affect them. This is often a one-way form of communication but critical for setting the stage for more interactive methods.

• Public Meetings: Organizing town halls or community forums to share information about an initiative. This method allows stakeholders to hear from project leaders and voice preliminary opinions.

• Newsletters and Bulletins: Regular updates through print or digital newsletters ensure the community remains informed.

• Social Media Campaigns: Platforms like Facebook, Twitter, and Instagram are increasingly used to disseminate information rapidly.

• Posters and Flyers: Visual materials placed in public spaces provide accessible and concise information.

While informative participation is a less interactive method, it establishes transparency and builds trust, encouraging further involvement.

2. Consultative Participation

In consultative participation, the community is engaged in providing feedback, often through structured methods that allow stakeholders to express their views on specific issues.

• Surveys and Questionnaires: Collecting quantitative and qualitative data from community members to understand their priorities and concerns.

• Focus Groups: Small, diverse groups discuss topics in-depth, enabling richer insights into community opinions and potential solutions.

• Public Hearings: Formal meetings where community members present their views to decision-makers, often used in urban planning and governance.

• Suggestion Boxes: Allowing anonymous feedback through physical or digital suggestion boxes ensures all voices can be heard.

Consultative participation ensures that community perspectives are incorporated into the decision-making process, even if they do not directly influence the outcomes.

3. Collaborative Participation

This method involves the community as active partners in planning, decision-making, and implementation. It emphasizes shared responsibility and mutual respect between stakeholders and the community.

• Participatory Rural Appraisal (PRA): Tools like mapping, transect walks, and seasonal calendars enable communities to assess their resources and identify priorities.

• Joint Committees: Forming committees with equal representation from community members and project teams ensures balanced decision-making.

• Workshops and Seminars: Interactive sessions where stakeholders collaborate to develop strategies and solutions.

• Co-Design and Co-Creation: Engaging the community in designing programs, products, or services that meet their specific needs.

Collaborative participation empowers communities by giving them a sense of ownership and responsibility, leading to more sustainable outcomes.

4. Empowering Participation

Empowering participation goes beyond collaboration, enabling communities to take control of projects and make autonomous decisions. It is the highest form of participation, fostering independence and self-reliance.

• Community-Led Development: Initiatives driven entirely by community members, with external stakeholders acting as facilitators or advisors.

• Capacity Building Programs: Training sessions and workshops enhance the community's skills and knowledge, preparing them to manage projects independently.

• Local Resource Mobilization: Encouraging communities to utilize and manage their resources effectively, reducing dependency on external funding.

• Participatory Budgeting: Allowing community members to decide how a portion of public or project funds should be allocated.

This method strengthens the community's ability to address challenges, promoting long-term resilience and self-sufficiency.

5. Advocacy-Based Participation

Advocacy-based participation focuses on empowering communities to voice their concerns, influence policies, and demand accountability from authorities.

• Awareness Campaigns: Educating communities about their rights and responsibilities through workshops, campaigns, and media.

• Grassroots Movements: Encouraging collective action through rallies, petitions, and lobbying efforts to bring about systemic change.

• Community Watch Groups: Establishing groups that monitor activities, such as environmental conservation or public service delivery, ensures accountability.

• Legal Aid and Support: Providing legal assistance to communities enables them to address grievances and assert their rights.

This method emphasizes the role of communities in shaping policies and governance structures to reflect their needs and aspirations.

6. Digital Participation

In the digital age, technology has become a vital tool for engaging communities. Digital participation methods are versatile, scalable, and can reach a diverse audience.

• Online Surveys and Polls: Quick and efficient tools for collecting feedback from a large number of participants.

• Webinars and Virtual Meetings: Facilitating discussions and knowledge-sharing among stakeholders and community members.

• Mobile Applications: Apps designed to engage communities in reporting issues, accessing services, or participating in decision-making.

• Crowdsourcing Platforms: Allowing communities to contribute ideas, resources, or data for projects.

Digital participation increases inclusivity by overcoming geographical and logistical barriers, making it easier for diverse groups to engage.

7. Cultural Participation

Cultural participation recognizes the importance of traditional practices, norms, and values in community engagement. It leverages cultural frameworks to foster meaningful interactions.

• Festivals and Celebrations: Using cultural events as platforms for raising awareness and promoting community initiatives.

• Storytelling and Theater: Employing traditional storytelling or theater performances to convey messages and encourage dialogue.

• Art and Music Workshops: Creative outlets for expressing community concerns and aspirations.

• Traditional Leadership Structures: Collaborating with elders or tribal leaders to ensure culturally sensitive and accepted practices.

By respecting and incorporating cultural elements, this method fosters deeper connections and trust within the community.

8. Educational Participation

Educational participation focuses on knowledge-sharing and equipping communities with the tools to engage meaningfully.

• Workshops and Training Programs: Providing targeted training in areas such as health, environment, or governance.

• Community Learning Centers: Establishing hubs for continuous learning and skill development.

• Youth Engagement Programs: Encouraging young people to take an active role in community development.

• Peer Education Models: Leveraging the influence of community members to educate and engage others.

Educational participation ensures that communities are well-informed and capable of contributing effectively to development processes.

9. Economic Participation

Economic participation involves integrating community members into economic activities that support development and provide livelihoods.

• Microfinance Initiatives: Offering small loans or financial services to empower community members economically.

• Income-Generating Projects: Encouraging participation in activities like agriculture, handicrafts, or small enterprises.
• Skill Development Programs: Training individuals in trades or professions that contribute to personal and community prosperity.
• Public-Private Partnerships: Collaborating with private sector entities to create job opportunities and foster economic growth.
This method strengthens the economic foundation of communities, enhancing their capacity to support development initiatives.

10. Spatial Participation

Spatial participation focuses on engaging communities in decisions about physical spaces, such as urban planning, housing, or infrastructure.
• Community Mapping: Involving residents in mapping their neighborhoods to identify challenges and opportunities.
• Participatory Zoning: Collaborating with communities to designate land use that aligns with their needs and aspirations.
• Design Charrettes: Intensive workshops where community members, planners, and designers co-create solutions for urban or rural spaces.
• Place-Making Activities: Engaging communities in creating public spaces that reflect their identity and needs.
This method ensures that the built environment aligns with the preferences and well-being of the community.

Challenges in Community Participation

Despite the benefits, community participation faces several challenges:
1. Limited Resources: Financial, human, and technical resources may be insufficient to support participation.
2. Power Imbalances: Dominance by certain groups can marginalize others, reducing inclusivity.
3. Cultural Barriers: Differences in language, norms, or values can hinder effective engagement.
4. Time Constraints: Participation processes can be time-consuming, deterring community involvement.
5. Lack of Trust: Historical grievances or failed initiatives may lead to skepticism.
Community participation is a dynamic and multifaceted process, with methods ranging from information dissemination to empowering communities to take control of their development. By choosing the appropriate method based on the context and objectives, stakeholders can foster inclusivity, sustainability, and resilience in community initiatives.

This diversity of methods ensures that community participation is not a one-size-fits-all approach but a flexible strategy tailored to meet specific needs. By overcoming challenges and continuously improving practices, community participation can unlock the full potential of collective action for a better future.

IV. Techniques of Participatory Rural Appraisal (PRA)

PRA techniques are tools to facilitate participatory learning and empower communities to contribute to development planning and decision-making. Below is a detailed elaboration of the key techniques:

1. Mapping and Diagramming

• Social Mapping:

This involves creating a visual representation of a community's layout, including houses, schools, clinics, and other facilities. It identifies social structures, caste systems, or economic classes. This helps in understanding resource distribution and areas of social exclusion.

Use: Identifying underserved areas or groups requiring intervention.

• Resource Mapping:

This focuses on the natural resources within a community, such as forests, water bodies, agricultural fields, and grazing lands. It provides insights into how resources are utilized and managed.

Use: Planning resource-based projects like water conservation or afforestation.

• Transect Walks:

Facilitators and community members take systematic walks through the community, observing and documenting land use, infrastructure, vegetation, and challenges. They interact with locals to understand spatial and environmental issues.

Use: Assessing resource availability and identifying problem areas.

2. Seasonal Calendars

Communities chart activities like planting, harvesting, festivals, migration, or weather patterns on a timeline. This visual tool helps understand fluctuations in labor, income, food availability, and vulnerabilities (e.g., droughts or floods).

Use: Scheduling interventions during low-stress periods, like lean agricultural months.

3. Time Lines and Historical Analysis

Participants narrate the history of their community, highlighting major events such as droughts, migrations, infrastructural developments, or conflicts. This builds a timeline of socio-economic and environmental changes.

Use: Understanding how past events shape current challenges and opportunities.

4. Wealth Ranking

Community members categorize households based on agreed-upon indicators like income, landholding, livestock, or housing quality. Rankings often reveal disparities in wealth and vulnerability within the community.

Use: Targeting support to the poorest or most vulnerable households.

5. Venn Diagrams

Participants draw diagrams to illustrate relationships between individuals, organizations, and institutions in their community. Circles of varying sizes and distances depict influence, importance, and interaction.

Use: Identifying key stakeholders, communication gaps, or power dynamics for better project collaboration.

6. Problem Ranking and Prioritization

Participants list issues affecting their community and rank them based on severity, frequency, or impact. This creates a clear hierarchy of problems, allowing focused action on priority issues.

Use: Ensuring that interventions address the most critical concerns.

7. Focus Group Discussions

Facilitators organize small, diverse groups to discuss specific issues in-depth. These discussions generate qualitative data, allowing for exploration of attitudes, opinions, and potential solutions.

Use: Gaining a deeper understanding of complex issues like gender roles or health practices.

8. Livelihood Analysis

Participants identify and evaluate various livelihood strategies, such as farming, fishing, or artisan work. The analysis considers factors like income, risks, sustainability, and barriers to livelihood improvement.

Use: Designing programs that enhance livelihood security and sustainability.

9. Trend Analysis

This technique captures changes in community practices, resources, or socio-economic conditions over time. Trends in agriculture, migration, deforestation, or disease prevalence are explored.

Use: Informing long-term planning and adaptive strategies.

10. Matrix Scoring and Pairwise Ranking

• **Matrix Scoring**: Participants create matrices to score and compare options (e.g., crops, technologies, or water sources) based on criteria such as cost, accessibility, or productivity.

• **Pairwise Ranking**: Options are compared in pairs to determine the most preferred or impactful choice.

Use: Supporting decision-making by objectively evaluating alternatives.

V. Guidelines for Social Impact Assessment (SIA)

Social Impact Assessment (SIA) is a process to evaluate the social effects of planned projects, programs, or policies. It identifies potential positive and negative impacts on communities and recommends strategies to enhance benefits and mitigate adverse effects. Below is a comprehensive guideline for conducting an effective SIA:

1. Define Objectives and Scope

• Purpose: Clearly define the objectives of the SIA, including what impacts will be assessed and why.

• Scope: Identify the geographical, temporal, and thematic boundaries of the assessment.

• Stakeholders: Determine the key stakeholders, including communities, government agencies, and organizations.

• Compliance: Align with relevant legal, institutional, and policy frameworks.

2. Stakeholder Engagement

• Participatory Approach: Involve affected communities, especially marginalized and vulnerable groups, throughout the process.

• Consultation: Use participatory techniques like focus groups, interviews, and public meetings to gather stakeholder inputs.

• Transparency: Share information openly about the project and SIA process.

3. Baseline Data Collection

• Social Profile: Gather data on the demographic, cultural, economic, and social characteristics of the affected communities.

• Key Indicators: Define and document baseline indicators, such as income levels, health conditions, education rates, and social infrastructure.

• Methods: Use both quantitative (surveys, census data) and qualitative (interviews, ethnographic studies) methods for comprehensive data collection.

4. Identify Potential Impacts

• Types of Impacts: Consider all direct, indirect, and cumulative impacts, including:

o Social cohesion and community relationships.

o Livelihoods and economic opportunities.

o Access to resources and services.

o Cultural heritage and identity.

o Health, safety, and well-being.

• Beneficial vs. Adverse Impacts: Differentiate between positive and negative effects and their magnitude, likelihood, and duration.

5. Predict and Analyze Impacts

• Impact Analysis: Use qualitative and quantitative tools to evaluate the significance and scale of identified impacts.

• Scenario Analysis: Develop alternative scenarios to understand varying project outcomes.

• Vulnerability Assessment: Identify how impacts disproportionately affect vulnerable groups (e.g., women, children, elderly, indigenous populations).

6. Develop Mitigation and Enhancement Strategies

• Mitigation Measures: Propose actions to minimize or eliminate negative impacts (e.g., relocation plans, compensation frameworks).

• Enhancement Strategies: Recommend measures to maximize the benefits of the project for local communities.

• Sustainability: Ensure the strategies align with long-term community development goals.

7. Prepare SIA Report

• Structure: Include the following sections:

1. Executive Summary.

2. Project Description.

3. Baseline Social Conditions.

4. Identified Impacts.

5. Mitigation and Enhancement Strategies.

6. Monitoring and Evaluation Plan.

7. Appendices (data, maps, references).

• Clarity: Use clear, non-technical language where possible to make the report accessible to all stakeholders.

8. Monitoring and Evaluation (M&E)

• Indicators: Develop measurable indicators to track the effectiveness of mitigation and enhancement strategies.

• Regular Monitoring: Implement a systematic plan to monitor social impacts during and after project implementation.

• Adaptive Management: Revise strategies based on feedback and changing conditions.

9. Ensure Compliance and Ethical Practices

• Regulatory Compliance: Adhere to all national and international SIA regulations and standards.

• Ethics: Respect cultural sensitivities, ensure informed consent, and avoid coercion or exploitation.

• Data Protection: Maintain confidentiality and protect the privacy of participants.

10. Continuous Stakeholder Communication

• Feedback Mechanism: Establish channels for continuous feedback from stakeholders during the project lifecycle.

• Grievance Redressal: Create a transparent and accessible system for addressing community concerns.

• Reporting: Provide periodic updates to stakeholders on the implementation of recommendations and the status of impacts.

A well-conducted SIA ensures that the social dimensions of development are integrated into decision-making processes. By following these guidelines, practitioners can promote equitable and sustainable development while mitigating risks to affected communities

VI. Guidelines for Environmental Impact Assessment (EIA)

Environmental Impact Assessment (EIA) is a systematic process used to evaluate the environmental consequences of proposed projects or policies before their implementation. It helps in decision-making by identifying potential environmental risks and ensuring sustainable development. Below are the key steps and guidelines for conducting an effective EIA:

1. Screening

• Purpose: Determine whether the proposed project requires an EIA and to what extent.

• Criteria: Use pre-defined thresholds or categories (e.g., project size, type, or location) to classify projects.

• Outcome: Decide if a full EIA is necessary, or if a simpler assessment like an Initial Environmental Examination (IEE) suffices.

2. Scoping

• Objective: Define the scope and boundaries of the EIA.

• Key Activities:

o Identify environmental aspects and potential impacts.

o Engage stakeholders to determine their concerns and priorities.

o Develop Terms of Reference (ToR) for the EIA study.

• Outcome: A clear focus on significant environmental issues.

3. Baseline Data Collection

• Purpose: Establish a comprehensive baseline of the current environmental conditions.

• Key Components:

o Physical environment: Climate, geology, water resources, air quality.

o Biological environment: Flora, fauna, ecosystems, biodiversity.

o Socio-economic environment: Population, livelihoods, cultural heritage.

• Methods: Use primary data (field surveys) and secondary data (existing reports and records).

4. Impact Identification and Prediction

• Types of Impacts: Consider direct, indirect, cumulative, and synergistic impacts across physical, biological, and socio-economic dimensions.

• Prediction Tools: Use models, GIS, and other tools to predict the magnitude, duration, and spatial extent of impacts.

• Key Areas:

o Air, water, and soil quality.

o Wildlife and habitat loss.

o Noise and vibration levels.

o Social and health impacts.

5. Mitigation Measures

• Objective: Propose measures to prevent, minimize, or compensate for adverse impacts.

• Hierarchy:

1. Avoidance: Prevent impacts altogether.

2. Minimization: Reduce the intensity or extent of impacts.

3. Compensation: Offset residual impacts through restoration or other means.

• Examples: Emission controls, reforestation, relocation of affected species, wastewater treatment.

6. Public Consultation and Participation

• Purpose: Ensure transparency and inclusivity in the decision-making process.

• Methods:

o Public hearings, workshops, focus groups, and surveys.

o Dissemination of information in local languages.

• Outcome: Integration of community concerns and suggestions into the

EIA report.

7. Environmental Management Plan (EMP)

• Components:

o Mitigation measures for identified impacts.

o Monitoring and compliance strategies.

o Institutional framework for implementation.

o Contingency plans for emergencies.

• Goal: Provide a practical framework for managing environmental risks during the project lifecycle.

8. Reporting

• Structure of EIA Report:

1. Executive Summary.

2. Introduction and Project Description.

3. Baseline Environmental Conditions.

4. Impact Assessment and Mitigation Measures.

5. Alternatives Analysis.

6. Environmental Management Plan (EMP).

7. Public Consultation Summary.

8. Conclusions and Recommendations.

• Clarity: Ensure the report is concise, well-structured, and accessible to non-technical stakeholders.

9. Decision-Making

• Objective: Provide authorities with a comprehensive understanding of environmental risks and benefits.

• Alternatives Analysis: Include options like no-project scenarios, alternative technologies, or locations.

• Approval Conditions: Specify mitigation and monitoring requirements as part of project approval.

10. Monitoring and Auditing

• Monitoring Plan: Define indicators, frequency, and methods for monitoring environmental impacts during and after project implementation.

• Compliance Audits: Verify adherence to mitigation measures and regulatory standards.

• Feedback Mechanism: Adjust mitigation strategies based on monitoring results.

11. Legal and Ethical Considerations

• Regulatory Compliance: Follow national EIA laws and international environmental agreements.

• Ethics: Ensure honesty, transparency, and respect for affected communities and ecosystems.

• Documentation: Maintain accurate and comprehensive records of all EIA activities.

12. Continuous Stakeholder Engagement

• Grievance Mechanism: Establish channels for stakeholders to voice concerns throughout the project lifecycle.

• Reporting Back: Provide regular updates on the implementation of mitigation measures and environmental performance.

An effective EIA ensures that environmental considerations are integrated into project planning and decision-making. By following these guidelines, developers, consultants, and regulators can promote sustainable development while minimizing ecological and social harm.

* 9 7 9 8 8 9 7 2 4 6 5 7 1 *